Web Design Templates Sourcebook

Lisa Schmeiser

Contributing HTML Template Developers:

Tori Copeland
Pearle Deanes
"Boy" Elroy Evertszoon
Jennifer Lawrence
Melanie Nelson
Brock Rumer

New Riders

New Riders Publishing, Indianapolis, Indiana

Web Design Templates Sourcebook

By Lisa Schmeiser

Published by:
New Riders Publishing
201 West 103rd Street
Indianapolis, IN 46290 USA

Printed in the United States of America 1 2 3 4 5 6 7 8 9 0

Library of Congress Cataloging-in-Publication Data

```
***CIP data available upon request***
```

Warning and Disclaimer

This book is designed to provide information about templates. Every effort has been made to make this book as complete and as accurate as possible, but no warranty or fitness is implied.

The information is provided on an "as is" basis. The author(s) and New Riders Publishing shall have neither liability nor responsibility to any person or entity with respect to any loss or damages arising from the information contained in this book or from the use of the disks or programs that may accompany it.

Associate Publisher	*David Dwyer*
Marketing Manager	*Mary Foote*
Managing Editor	*Carla Hall*
Director of Development	*Kezia Endsley*

Product Development Specialist
David Gibson

Acquisitions Editor
Steve Weiss

Senior Editors
Sarah Kearns
Suzanne Snyder

Development Editor
Christopher Cleveland

Project Editor
Gina Brown

Copy Editors
Jennifer Clark
Michelle Warren

Technical Editor
Kim Scott

Software Specialist
Steve Flatt

**Software Acquisitions
and Development**
Dustin Sullivan

Assistant Marketing Manager
Gretchen Schlesinger

Acquisitions Coordinator
Stacey Beheler

Editorial Assistant
Karen Opal

Manufacturing Coordinator
Brook Farling

Cover Designer
Louisa Klucznik

Cover Production
Aren Howell

Book Designer
Glenn Larsen

Director of Production
Larry Klein

Production Team Supervisors
Laurie Casey
Joe Millay

Graphics Image Specialists
Steve Adams
Wil Cruz
Oliver Jackson

Production Analysts
Dan Harris
Erich J. Richter

Production Team
Kim Cofer, Tricia Flodder, Linda Knose

Indexer
Joe Long

About the Author(s)

Lisa Schmeiser's web career includes stints at Rensselaer Polytechnic Institute, the American Association for the Advancement of Science, and *HotWired*. She is currently working at CNet, in the creative services department. She has written for a number of online publications, including the online pioneer in the genre, *Computer Mediated Communication Magazine*. Lisa has also been interviewed by every major paper in Philadelphia, despite never having set foot in that city. She earned her B.S. in biology from Virginia Polytechnic Institute and State University, and her M.S. in technical communication from Rensselaer Polytechnic Institute. Her future goals include earning a Ph.D. at yet another academic institution with polytechnic in the name.

Trademark Acknowledgments

All terms mentioned in this book that are known to be trademarks or service marks have been appropriately capitalized. New Riders Publishing cannot attest to the accuracy of this information. Use of a term in this book should not be regarded as affecting the validity of any trademark or service mark.

Dedications

In memory of Rudolph Schmeiser.

Acknowledgments

From Lisa Schmeiser:

It may be my name on the cover, but this book is real, live proof of concerted teamwork. It would not have been written without the expert aid of the people mentioned here, all of whom unselfishly contributed time and talent to this project.

First and foremost, thanks to my editor Steve Weiss, whose well-timed e-mail set the ball rolling on this book. Steve's patience, persistence, and constant encouragement surely qualify him for some sort of humanitarian award.

Props and kudos to the ever-patient development staff at New Riders: Gina Brown, Chris Cleveland, and David Gibson. Their collective eye for detail, knack for organizing vast amounts of information, and free meals are what pulled the book together.

This book would not have been finished without the talented template development team; each of them contributed time and energy in helping to create the more than 300 templates in this book, and their assistance was invaluable.

Thanks also to my co-workers at *HotWired*, whose understanding and cooperation ensured that I had time to write: Rick Boyce, Bryan Lurie, Rachel Wight, and Danaa Zellers were superlative colleagues among an organization filled with extraordinary people.

Finally, thanks to my friends, whose support and encouragement prevented me from buying a firearm and using it on my CPU. Heartfelt thanks goes to my family for their support, and for not noticing that I only called home when I had writer's block.

From New Riders Publishing:

New Riders would like to thank the following people: Rich Evers, Mark Matthews, Kim Scott, Ian Smith, and Marvin Van Tiem.

Contents at a Glance

Contents

Introduction

Templates

The word "template" doesn't seem too exciting at first: it implies unoriginality and boring sameness. Nothing could be further from the truth. Templates enable you to be creative, and to accomplish more innovative work. The key is where you channel that creativity. This book will show you that templates aren't a recipe for mind-numbing web site conformity, but a flexible tool that allows you to design, build, and maintain innovative and functional web sites.

Still not convinced? Templates give you free time. Barring superhuman endurance or a bite from one of those "funny" bats, the allure of staying up all night to do detail-oriented work wears off after a while. Templates enable you to crank out 50 pages of content daily and still make it home before Nick at Nite. Templates are a checklist and shortcut rolled into one: you can crank out those 50 pages, go home, and channel surf without the nagging worry that you forgot an essential user interface element, like a page title. Templates provide you with a way to rapidly apply new web development technologies across a site, and to incorporate new content into an existing web site as seamlessly as possible.

In short, templates accomplish two admirable goals: first, they help you to work more efficiently. In an industry where rapid technological development is outpaced only by the rate of web content publishing, any step that saves you time helps.

Second, templates help you to develop and maintain a modicum of smart user interface design across your site. Templates can help you set up and maintain a site that is not only attractive but functional with a minimal amount of upkeep. In a medium where ease of use is as big a draw as quality of content, a good user interface will win you a wide audience.

What Is the Value and Importance of this Book?

The goal of this book is to give you a boost from work-induced catatonia into efficient web production. It's meant to offer ideas, or possibly a little instruction, that you can use to begin building a web site. This book offers several organizational strategies that can help you translate reams of prose into a dynamic, yet navigable web site; several tenets of basic user interface design and application are introduced and repeated (and repeated) throughout the book. I've grouped complementary UI principles and suggested methods of organization in different chapters, and each chapter is geared toward a particular type of web site.

Why compartmentalize? It's an organizational strategy: step one of moving out of work catatonia.

This book is also a good how-to for those of you who are building your first big web site, or just beginning to manage web site development. I have written about UI and organization, but I also back up what I say with annotated examples. You can learn by doing, not by reading an obtuse paragraph and trying to figure out how it might apply to your project.

How this Book Is Organized

Web Design Templates Sourcebook is composed of eight chapters.

Chapter 1, Why Would You Need this Book?

This chapter outlines even more reasons to use this book, in case my argument here isn't convincing enough. Chapter 1 outlines the web development cycle and trys to render a chaotic and fluid process into something that you can control and use intelligently.

Chapter 2, Skills Primer

Here's where the type of HTML background you'll need to get the most out of the book is provided. Although this is not a complete catalog of every HTML command known to humankind, I do explain the ideas of functional and structural HTML. I also explain and illustrate what different tags are and how they're used. Other chapter bonuses: an exhaustive list of brainstorming questions that will help define the process you'll use to build your web site, and a quick graphics tutorial.

Chapter 3, Text-Heavy Materials

The first template-intensive chapter discusses the process behind translating wordy materials to the one-screen-at-a-time medium. Chapter 3 focuses on reports, articles, groups of articles, and directories; all the web sites are geared toward presenting an organized, information-intensive structure. The templates in this chapter center around text; to use them you'll need to exercise some editorial judgment, set up a navigation system within your content, and drop the pieces into place.

Chapter 4, Frequently-Updated Contents

This chapter discusses ways to conquer the Sisyphean task of constantly updating a web site: we discuss information triaging strategies and demonstrate templates that act as a flexible site skeleton for ever-changing content. News-intensive sites, online calendars, and searchable indices all fall into this category.

Chapter 5, Corporate/Promotional Web Sites

Chapter 5 discusses the balancing act between web-specific design and company-mandated design. The templates demonstrate how to incorporate and maintain a company's distinctive visual trademarks with widely recognizable UI features. Annual reports, business plans and prospecti, and media kits are all highlighted here.

Chapter 6, Forms

The templates here focus on hosting an information exchange as painlessly as possible. Please note: the chapter focuses on organizing and presenting material; it does not provide backend scripting to parse data input.

Chapter 7, Multifunctional Sites

This chapter discusses strategies for combining multiple content-driven functions into one coherent web site. To translate: you'll see how to create a site that can pull together search interfaces, short and long articles, and a company-driven area.

Chapter 8, Alternatives to HTML Templates

Web development moves extremely rapidly, and this chapter discusses post-HTML strategies like automation, dynamic HTML, and other mechanized approaches to producing a large web site without a lot of human work.

Accessing and Customizing Templates from the CD-ROM

All the templates and related source files are located on the CD-ROM in the respective project folders for each chapter. If, for example, you're looking for the template called 3_i_02, you would look in the following directory: d:/projects/03tmplts/3_i_02.htm. Double-click on the HTML file. The file will open in the program that you have associated with .htm/.html files. You can also edit the templates using your favorite text editor or in Notepad.

When you've made changes to the template to suit your task, save the modified HTML file to your hard drive and make sure that any images that you've changed are placed in the same directory.

New Riders Publishing

The staff of New Riders Publishing is committed to bringing you the very best in computer reference material. Each New Riders book is the result of months of work by authors and staff who research and refine the information contained within its covers.

As part of this commitment to you, New Riders invites your input. Please let us know if you enjoy this book, if you have trouble with the information and examples presented, or if you have a suggestion for the next edition.

Please note, however: New Riders staff cannot serve as a technical resource for templates or for questions about software- or hardware-related problems. Please refer to the documentation that accompanies your software or to the applications' Help systems.

If you have a question or comment about any New Riders book, there are several ways to contact us. We will respond to as many readers as we can. Your name, address, or phone number will never become part of a mailing list or be used for any purpose other than to help us continue to bring you the best books possible.

You can write us at the following address:

New Riders Publishing
Attn: Publisher
201 W. 103rd Street
Indianapolis, IN 46290

If you prefer, you can fax New Riders Publishing at:

317-817-7448

You can also send electronic mail to New Riders at the following Internet address:

`sweiss@newriders.mcp.com`

New Riders Publishing is an Imprint of Macmillan Computer Publishing. To obtain a catalog or information, or to purchase any Macmillan Computer Publishing book, call 800-428-5331 or visit our web site at `http://www.mcp.com`.

Thank you for selecting *Web Design Templates Sourcebook*!

CHAPTER 1

Why Would You Need this Book?

What this chapter covers:

❖ Why Is this Book Important?

❖ Why Should You Buy this Book?

❖ An Argument for HTML Templates—the Modus Operandi of the Book

Why Is this Book Important?

Wait! Before you put this book down and dismiss it as yet another web publishing book, take a minute and read why this book even exists.

This book and accompanying CD-ROM exist as a dual resource for building dynamic web sites with as little work as possible.

That's not to say that building a web site isn't going to involve work: it's a question of knowing where to concentrate your efforts, and at what point in the site-building process you'll have to concentrate those efforts. That's not to say there isn't some work—it's just a question of knowing when to do it, and where to concentrate your time and resources. This book can help you do this, and make the process of building a web site more manageable. It will also make the posted product one that you're proud to display. You can build good sites systematically, without having them look like the end result of some dictator's five-year plan.

In addition, this book doesn't treat building web sites as a finite process. The blessing and bane of the digital medium is the ease and rapidity with which you can make changes to material. As you or your bosses catch on to how easy it is to expand your web site, you'll be adding more content until even you lose track of where specific content files reside. Then it will be time to redesign the site, reorganize it, and rebuild it—even those content files lost in the depths of your directory tree.

A smart way exists to untangle and makeover a legacy web site, and smart ways exist to prevent those web sites from happening. This book will share some of them with you, and give you the tools to think of individual, creative solutions to similar problems.

In other words, this book recognizes that building good web sites isn't just an intuitive art—it is a learned craft. You'll learn the basic tools of that craft, giving you the know-how to take these tools and use them to manage and build a plethora of various web sites.

Why Should You Buy this Book?

You should buy this book because, like any useful tool, it's more useful when it's immediately at hand. You should also buy this book because it provides more than laundry lists of proven strategies for building great web sites. It gives you a new way of looking at the clusters of files that comprise web sites.

Think of it this way: the web is often referred to as a world of its own. As a web site producer, you're contributing directly to the digital ecology. The way you choose to fence in your content or shovelware, the file formats, and layout decisions you make will affect your small part of the web. And it will affect the world web in a larger sense—you've just contributed something to the rapid, unchecked growth of web pages out there.

Like any ecological system, nothing stands alone on the web. You're probably aware of the process for nurturing your site externally—attracting and keeping traffic, promoting the content on your site to others, and engaging in hypertext symbiosis with other sites in the hopes of sharing the limited resource of readers. But internal processes go into building a web site as a strong, competitive creation in the crowded digital jungle.

These processes go beyond simple how-tos and the steps for building an individual web page. To build a site that is structurally sound and elegant, easy to update, and not overly labor-intensive takes planning. It requires solid answers to a barrage of questions, some theoretical, some practical.

The theoretical questions concern the purpose and goals behind your web site, such as:

- ❖ What does your web site have to offer a web surfer?
- ❖ How do you plan on taking advantage of the flexible protocols that govern web development?

The specific questions, after they are answered, take the web site from a proposal to a set of files ready for posting. The answers to these questions shape the look and feel of your interface and determine what behind-the-scenes tools you'll use to manage the site:

- ❖ What is the lowest technological barrier you can set for your audience? Who is your target audience?
- ❖ What type of information are you offering on your web site? How will you use hypertext to present it?
- ❖ How will you deal with the challenge of not being able to control the technology and software your viewer will be using?

If you're reading these questions and you find yourself scrambling for answers, this book can help. The goal of this book is to present the construction of a quality web site as a series of processes, and to offer a way to select construction processes that are best suited for the site that you're going to build.

The Constants of Web Development

This book focuses on the constants in web site development:

- ❖ Site structure
- ❖ Navigation
- ❖ Layout
- ❖ Content presentation

As you read through the suggested process for building a web site, you'll learn what the role of each of these elements is in the development of a site, and how each element influences the finished product.

This book also shows you how to exploit these elements for a more efficient web-building experience. Ultimately, tackling the basics first allows you more time to explore the latest graphics and stylistic trends. Think of it this way: you begin building a web site, going only on a content-driven outline and a rough mock-up from a designer. You have your hands full learning and applying the latest technologies and updating your pages to retain an audience.

Determining which web development strategies work best for building the site and which strategies work best for maintaining the site take time. The backend organizational work, the rounds of layout revisions, and the cross-platform testing are also time-consuming. When will you handle going back and revising 60 pages when you realize that you forgot to build a working hyperlink in the Home button?

This book can help you remember to build a web site structure that eliminates small, annoying, widespread gaffes. Throughout this book, you'll learn to make building, updating, or correcting web pages as efficient and accurate as possible. You'll also be provided with a few suggestions for reducing the overall number of small and annoying errors.

Generating Appealing Content

Some of the content in this book shows you how to exploit the web medium and bring your readers a web site experience that they'll remember. This is a goal worth striving for! Most web sites are made or broken via word-of-mouth, whether that word comes by e-mail, hyperlink, or old media coverage. If you have a strong web site, there's a strong chance you'll have the continued opportunity to build or maintain sites.

Some of the content in this book also deals with human-computer interface in a real, practical way. A list of common-sense questions is provided in Chapter 2, "Skills Primer"—these will enable you to determine what counts on your site and how to transmit that to an audience that you may not know much about. You'll learn how to apply the overarching goal of HCI—make the technology invisible to the user—to your web site without compromising the technical potential that your site has.

You can jumpstart your creativity just by flipping through this book. Brainstorming—as messy, loud, and disorderly as it is—is a time-honored way of starting a project. Brainstorming enables you to articulate and bounce ideas off other people, and to begin cogitating on how they may work. This book is no substitute for a roomful of people, but if you're stuck in front of a blank monitor, in an empty office, pick up this book. Page through the templates provided throughout the book. Find features you like—it doesn't matter if those features are on the same web layout or not, you're brainstorming. Ask yourself how your content would fit on a different design. How would you modify it? What would you change?

Begin noting what you do and don't like. Within a reasonable time span, you'll be generating an original interface. The templates in this book are here to provide you with inspiration. They're here to provide smart HTML how-tos. They're here to demonstrate the four basic tenets of web building: site structure, navigation, layout, and content presentation. They're here for you.

An Argument for HTML Templates—the Modus Operandi of the Book

Two factors affecting the way people build web sites today are:

❖ The boom in web site–producing software products

❖ Increased emphasis on dynamic, customizable content

Both factors pull the web site producer away from the earlier meaning of the job: someone who used a basic-level text markup "language" to push content into a screen-appropriate layout and post it to the web.

That's not to say the change is bad. Software that does the HTML behind the scenes enables a web site producer to focus on the overall look and feel of the interface. HTML has been evolving to meet the dual challenges of denoting an information structure (the equivalent of setting up an outline) and providing attractive layout options, but kludges are still common, and this software puzzles those out for you. Also, drawing chunks of content from a database and dropping them into preformatted pieces of code (also generated by script) eliminates the need to have a large human staff churning out new pages in response to fast deadlines or late posting deadlines. It also eliminates the probability that one overworked human is trying to post frequently, or reliably, with a minimum of error.

These "new" methods of creating and publishing web content are a natural development in the content development model of the web: fast, small-staffed, and lightweight. They also represent the way content and design are currently viewed on the web, and the way they are treated in the book: as elements that can be mixed and matched to create a dynamic whole.

Drawbacks to Automating Web Content

Unfortunately, there are tradeoffs to web content mechanization. Buggy databases or clunky layout programs aside, the tools for mass-producing sites are still missing a vital element—human judgment. Although it's possible to assign specific data values or categories to each element in a web page, drawbacks exist to neatly compartmentalize web page pieces. First, there will always be exceptions to the rule—how does the database deal with these? Second, any site expansion, reorganization, or redesign will call for a corresponding change in the database. How does that affect the existing site? Will it mean doubling resources while the site is in transition?

Another tradeoff in the increasing mechanization of web publishing is the shift in skills and resources required to run the site. Software that is meant to reduce the time and work on a project may add to it in unexpected ways. How much technical knowledge is required to maintain or troubleshoot the web site? Does it require learning a new set of skills or importing an expert? How do these skills impact the amount of time or personnel put on the content and design aspects of the web site?

A third tradeoff to increasing web publishing mechanization is a drop in the impact of *cause-and-effect coding*. Cause-and-effect coding isn't new jargon—it's a way to say that, for every software application that reduces the amount of direct work you do with a given chunk of information (be it visual, numeric, or text)—the less you know about the process and what it's doing to your information.

This isn't always a bad thing. In theory, software exists to provide a user with tools that enable him to work faster and more effectively. A lot of software does that, and works very well, especially if it provides an interface that permits the user to do tasks effectively and comfortably; however, this software usually works within a specific computer environment. Applications are written to work with, and take specific advantage of, a computer's operating system and desktop interface. The web is a whole different matter.

Remember that when you're designing and building a web site, no absolute guarantees to the speed of someone's web connection, monitor sizes, or resolutions exist. The software used to view a web page may only recognize HTML 2.0, or the user may be viewing the web pages with the images turned off. In other words, you have little control over the user's environment. You can write server-side workarounds for computer operating systems, software packages, or geographic parameters, but that adds to the server response time and raises technical issues outside the scope of this book's topic.

Making Web Content Mechanization Work for You

From a design and content development perspective, the diversity of software and hardware options presents a very real challenge: How do you build a product that carries well across the myriad of possible audience-technology combinations?

The first step toward finding a solution to that challenge is to have a thorough understanding of the elements that control the final product. In this case, to have a thorough understanding of what different HTML tags do, and how they can be used.

Web software packages often eliminate the need to learn precisely what each HTML tag does, and whether its function is more structural or spatial. Consequently, the <DL> kludge used to cleverly shift chunks of text around graphics wreaks havoc when displayed in some browsers. In addition, the farther removed the designer is from the behind-the-scenes language that will take the design online, the less control he has over fine-tuning the design.

More importantly, the less HTML-literate a designer is, the greater the possibility that the design's integral HTML does not reflect and reinforce the informational structure of the web site. This can have far-reaching repercussions when it's time to reorganize or redesign the site. This is why this book stresses a thorough knowledge of HTML and what it can and cannot do.

This doesn't mean this book is an elaborate argument against hand-built web sites: the templates in this book are designed to be pulled apart into chunks of functional HTML to be mixed, matched, rendered as macros, entered as database fields, or otherwise processed. Instead, this book introduces and reinforces some tenets of web design assumed to be common sense or common knowledge, including:

❖ Structural HTML tags and their corresponding values in an information structure.

❖ The elements that mark good interactive design: clear entries and exits, a list of contents, opportunity for feedback.

❖ Spatial arrangements that maximize structural tags and allow an easy reading experience.

Validating HTML Templates

HTML templates are used for several reasons. First, HTML is the lingua franca of the web. Understanding it doesn't require previous programming experience. It is the building block of web pages; you couldn't ask for a clearer demonstration of cause-and-effect programming. Start with the premise that a correctly entered markup tag will perform a specific and visual function. Say you wanted to include a hypertext link in your document. You would enter the anchor tag, the item you wanted linked, and the closing anchor tag: <A HREF="">item</A>. If you incorrectly enter the anchor tag—typing <A HREF"">—the link will not show at all. If you forget the closing tag, it consumes the page. Such visual cues aren't only a not-so-subtle clue that you made a mistake, they're also a handy way to troubleshoot your HTML. Figure 1.1 shows correct and incorrect examples of hyperlinks.

Figure 1.1

A plain hyperlink versus hyperlink-gone-pagewide.

In the bottom paragraph of figure 1.1, you see a broken hyperlink that's affected the content on the entire page. The top sentence in figure 1.1 shows the link correctly set up. Seeing what happened in the bottom paragraph is as easy as going to your browser's View Source option and noting that the code reads:

```
<<a href = "foo.html "The quick brown fox jumped over the lazy dog. The quick
brown fox jumped over the lazy dog. The quick brown fox jumped over the lazy
dog. The quick brown fox jumped over the lazy dog.
```

and fixing it to read:

```
<a href= "foo.html"> The quick brown fox</a> jumped over the lazy dog. The quick
brown fox jumped over the lazy dog. The quick brown fox jumped over the lazy
dog. The quick brown fox jumped over the lazy dog.
```

The fix may not be intuitive at first, but a few hours of reviewing the markup nature of HTML (effects are typically closed in beginning and ending brackets) and you'll see exactly how hypertext affects content and presentation.

So HTML is the perfect common ground for the examples set forth in this book—beginning web site designers can apply the layout tricks demonstrated with the same facility as experienced web producers.

But why templates? Doesn't that compress any originality into cookie-cutter molds?

Not necessarily. Templates don't have to be the final word on what the web site is going to look like. They're the tool used in this book to demonstrate how to approach a large and intangible project, analyze what the site is going to do and how it's going to do it, and then break the project into easily manageable chunks.

Templates do this by setting up and providing a structured environment for project management. After you hammer out answers to basic questions (a list of which you'll see in Chapter 2, "Skills Primer") and commit to an information and design structure, you can sort and prioritize the various parts of your project based on where they fit in that framework. Consequently, that's less time spent staring glassy-eyed at the huge project you're to turn out on a constraining deadline.

Organization often leads to more efficient work (assuming you don't become enthralled with the organization process), thus saving you time. Templates can also make it easier to stick to a set timetable, especially one that doesn't leave a lot of room for revision. As your site continues to grow, or the content changes on a frequent basis, or you add increasing user interactivity, you'll have more to think about than whether or not you remembered to include a Back button on the bottom of every page. Taking the time to build a strong template—one that includes all the elements that should be on a large web site—will ultimately reduce the time you would have to take in tracking down and correcting small and random errors.

This leads to the next point: Templates break web pages into discrete parts behind the scenes. If you need to do a massive, site-wide revision of the navigation tool, it's as easy as writing a search-and-replace for a specific chunk of code, in lieu of opening and checking every file.

This approach works especially well on sites that are large and growing; sites with a big emphasis on hyperlinking to intraweb content; or sites that are frequently updated. This part-whole approach is also a solution that enables your site to move easily to a script-and-database driven creation while letting you fine-tune pieces of your interface, troubleshoot bothersome code, or fix errors without overhauling the entire directory. In other words—templates enable you to respond to new ways of building and delivering content by giving you a flexible framework with which to begin.

Conclusion

Templates are a great way to jumpstart your creativity. A spam circulating on the Net says the solution to all management crises is to ask, "What would Batman do?" This book is a loose equivalent—if you're absolutely stumped or overwhelmed, just ask what we did. Within minutes you'll be appropriating, critiquing, reconstructing, or brainstorming your way to a solution that works for your content.

CHAPTER 2

Skills Primer

What this chapter covers:

- ❖ The Process of Building a Web Site
- ❖ Design—Form Versus Function?
- ❖ HTML Basics
- ❖ Text Browser Work-Arounds
- ❖ Conditional HTML
- ❖ Graphics

The Process of Building a Web Site

Building a web site is often a complicated process. You're responsible for pulling together content, graphics, a page layout, and backend applications seamlessly, on short notice. In that kind of rush, it's easy to forget about the people who are going to look at your finished product, who have no idea what you were thinking as you built it.

The people who are looking at your web site are the humans you often hear about in the phrase human-computer interaction. You're building your web site for these people on some level, whether as an archive or as a fully interactive service. Although a lot of work has been done to make computers more approachable for a wide audience, the kind of standardization that enables a person to recognize and use certain interface elements hasn't quite established itself on the web. This is where you pick up the slack.

No web site will ever be 100 percent clear to every user who hits it, but you can do a few things to ensure that your project reaches the largest possible audience. This chapter begins with the principles behind building a usable web site, and then moves on to the building blocks that you'll use to produce a web site.

Determine Site Usability

The first major consideration when building a web site is to commit to making it a usable web site. Decide what information that you are posting is usable, and brainstorm ways to build your site so that it highlights that usable quality. But note—information alone does not make a usable web site. What really works is usable information as part of a larger product. A site containing the following, for example:

❖ london.gif
❖ chicago.gif
❖ metro.gif
❖ nyc.gif
❖ bart.gif

might contain something a user is looking for, like a map of the New York City subway system, or it might overlook providing the user with this information. A site that looks like figure 2.1 tells the user what sort of information is available to her. After you've figured this out, you've got a loose content organizational structure.

Figure 2.1

A simple demonstration of organizing information for the user.

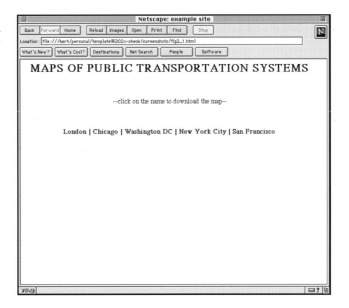

Targeting Your Audience

After you've decided what information is important, you need to figure out why people will visit your site. According to interface expert Ed Weiss, people have four reasons for seeking out information:

- ❖ They're motivated to
- ❖ They need the information to orient themselves
- ❖ They're looking for instruction and guidance
- ❖ They're looking for a reference work

Your site will likely provide one of the latter three reasons to visit—but what about motivating people to visit? Think of ways to combine motivation with orientation, reference, or instructions. These ways will influence the elements that you choose for your site's look and feel.

Increasing Site Accessibility

Next, decide how to make your site more accessible. This will help increase the motivation that others have to visit your site. If users feel comfortable looking for information, they'll be back. You can always make your site accessible by eliminating anything that you perceive as being too complicated or confusing for your visitors, but that reduces the reasons to visit your site in the long run. Instead, focus on making all your information accessible—expand the user's expectations of your site and provide the user with a way to feel as though he gained something from visiting your site. Begin with your user's previous knowledge and ease into unfamiliar territory. This is a good time to brainstorm elements of your web site that you feel users will recognize and use to explore your product.

Determine Site/User Interactivity

Finally, decide how interactive you're going to make the site. Now that we've emphasized the human part of human-computer interface, let's take a look at the rest of the phrase: How much control over the web site experience will the user have, and how much of that is determined by the interface? Deciding how your user will interact with the content, and to what degree, can help you to solidify the backend, content organization, and the navigation devices that you provide.

The Basic Guidelines for Building Web Sites

To sum up the previous four sections, consider these four points when building a web site:

❖ The information the user will find valuable
❖ The reason the user visits the site
❖ How you will make the site accessible to the user
❖ What degree of interactivity your site will have

Questions to Ask When Building a Web Site

To help you apply the basic guidelines sketched out in the previous sections to very real web projects, the following sections should be used as a checklist of considerations to be made prior to building a web site.

 TIP **Answer these questions as honestly as possible. You probably know more about this project than anyone else, and you're the only one who's going to see the answers.**

Value of Information

❖ What sort of information can you post on your web site?
❖ How can you make users take notice of important information?
❖ How does this information enhance your web site?
❖ How complex is this information?
❖ How do you plan on communicating that complexity to visitors?

Raison d'etre

- ❖ Why will people visit your web site?
  - ◆ It will teach them how to do something they don't know how to do.
  - ◆ It will be an introduction to an exciting new skill, hobby, or discipline.
  - ◆ It will be an introduction to an exciting new product or company.
  - ◆ It will have reference materials that they can use in everyday life.
  - ◆ It will have reference materials that they can use to learn more about a subject they already study or follow.
  - ◆ It will feature an exciting new application or game.
  - ◆ Other: (Fill in your own reasons)
- ❖ Who do you want to visit your web site?
- ❖ Who would you want to avoid your web site, if anyone?
- ❖ What will people gain from visiting your web site (think back to why they want to visit, and what happens at the end of a successful visit)?
- ❖ Will a user instantly gain something from visiting or are repeat visits necessary?

Accessibility

- ❖ How will you familiarize users with the content of your web site?
- ❖ How much effort will your strategy take for the users?
- ❖ How much of your strategy relies on users' previous knowledge?
- ❖ How much of your strategy relies on knowledge that you and your user share?
- ❖ What constraints will you apply to the information you're putting on the site?
- ❖ Try to find direct correlations between the information that you're including on the web site and the reasons a user would have for visiting your site. What matches up, and what is left out? Are those items necessary?
- ❖ What sort of user errors are you anticipating? How can you provide alternate methods of using the web site?
- ❖ What standards, if any, can you apply to your web site?
- ❖ How familiar do you want to make each web visit for your users?

Interactivity

- ❖ Who controls the web site point-and-click experience more?
- ❖ Have you mapped out the possible ways your user can visit and absorb the contents of your site? Are there any routes you want to eliminate? Add?

❖ How clearly do you state the limits of the web site's interactivity?

❖ How clearly do you state the equipment or skills the visitor needs to have the fullest web site experience?

❖ Have you provided an alternative interactive path for users who do not have the equipment or skills?

❖ How much interactivity do you have on your site?

❖ How is the interactivity paced? (Think of those choose-your-own-adventure books when you were a kid—didn't you hate reading page after page with no choices, and then having to make five decisions in a row?)

❖ What sort of narrative tone will you try to establish for your users? Personal? Irreverent? Organized? Removed (there is no human at this web site…)?

Design—Form Versus Function?

HTML tags fall within two distinct groups—functional tags and formatting tags. Functional tags are the meat-and-potatoes of the HTML. You use functional tags to build a reliable, usable structure for your web page. _Functional tags_ can set up an information hierarchy, establish the parts of your web page, and ensure that the basic page design is consistent from browser to browser.

Formatting tags control the appearance, not the structure, of the document. These tags are used to fine-tune the font sizes, color schemes, and element placement that visual designers want to carry over to their web sites.

Recent HTML specifications have addressed the need to have more aesthetic control over the content of a web site. When the last major version of HTML—HTML 3.0—was introduced, the W3 consortium wrote:

> "HTML is designed to allow rendering on a very wide range of devices, from clunky teletypes, to terminals, DOS, Windows, Macs and high end Workstations, as well as non-visual media such as speech and braille. In this, it allows users to exploit the legacy of older equipment as well as the latest and best of new machines. The experience with proprietary document formats has shown the dangers of mixing presentation markup with content (or structural) markup".

Consequently, there are tags in HTML 3.2 that specify formatting by linking a particular characteristic to a structural element. This is a big improvement. Designers can maintain more precise visual control without sacrificing readability across different browsers and platforms. The following two sections provide tables with detailed descriptions of the functional and formatting HTML tags.

Functional Tags

<HEAD></HEAD>	This paired tag sets up the head of the .html file.
<TITLE></TITLE>	This paired tag lists the title of the .html file as determined by you.
<BODY></BODY>	Anything within these tags, such as a background, is displayed in your browser window—the body of the web page.
<H1></H1> <H2></H2> <H3></H3> <H4></H4> <H5></H5> <H6></H6>	These are heading tags, listed here in order from largest to smallest. They're good for providing a visual means of sorting information hierarchically, such as building an outline.
<P>	This tag provides a one-space paragraph break.
<HR>	This tag is a one-pixel horizontal rule across a web site.
<BLOCKQUOTE></BLOCKQUOTE>	This paired tag indents a section of text. Blockquote tags can also be used to set up a left-hand margin that works in Netscape, thus giving it a formatting tag use as well as a functional tag use. In Internet Explorer, however, the blockquoted text will appear italicized.
<UL> <LI></LI> </UL>	These are the tags for unordered lists—the <UL> tags signify the beginning and end of the list, and the <LI> tags mark a new item in the list. Items are indicated via bullets.
<OL> <LI></LI> </OL>	These are the tags for a numbered list. Instead of bullet points, items are numbered 1–X.
<DL> <DT> <DD></DD> </DL>	These are tags for a definition list that indicates and formats a series of items and their corresponding data. These are another set of tags that, although initially serving a hierarchical purpose, can also be used for layout tweaks. Think of it this way: <DL></DL> tells the browser to expect a list <DT> definition title—this is the item that is set to the left of the definition entry. <DD></DD> sets up the beginning and end of the definition data by indenting it from the <DT>.
<CITE></CITE>	The citation tag indicates functionally that content needs to be set apart, usually via italics.

continued

<EM></EM>	The emphasis tag indicates functionally that the content needs to be given greater typographic emphasis; browsers typically translate this by applying bold to the text.
<TABLE> <TT></TT> <TR> <TD></TD> </TR> </TABLE>	A table, in three simple tags. The <TABLE> tags signify when the table begins and ends; <TT> sets the title of the table; the <TR> tags indicate the beginning and ends of rows within the table, and the <TD> tags enclose the individual cells within a table row.

Formatting Tags

 	This tag tells the browser to insert a line break. There's no indication structurally whether this is the start of a new paragraph, or just a way to make sure a very long sentence looks visually blocked.
<ALIGN = left> <ALIGN = right> <ALIGN = center> <ALIGN = top> <ALIGN = bottom>	The hypertext solution for lining up one HTML element relative to others.
TABLE formatting tags	These tags don't affect the structural organization of the table, but do interesting things to the visual arrangement of the table. Note also that these are added to structural tags.
<BORDER = N> where N = a numeral value from 0 on up.	This specifies the border that appears around all the different elements in your table. The default setting is border = 1; if you're using tables for layout purposes, you will want to set the border = 0, so that the elements appear evenly spaced, but not hemmed in by a border.
<COLLAPSING = N> where N = a numeral value from 0 on up.	The difference between cellpadding and cellspacing is where any visual separation of elements takes place: in cellpadding, the contents of an individual cell are surrounded by N pixels of space, and in cellspacing, the cells are separated from each other by N pixels of space.
<CELLSPACING = N> where N = a numeral value from 0 on up.	Cellspacing separates the actual table cells by inserting N pixels of space around the outside of the cell. Cellpadding places the pixel space on the inside.

<VALIGN = left/right/center> <HALIGN = left/right/center>	Added into <TD> or <TR> tags, these tags align the contents enclosed to the direction specified in the tag.
	With <TR VALIGN = left>, all the <TD> cells and contents of that cell would be left-aligned. Specifying <TD VALIGN = left> means only the contents of that table cell will be left-aligned.
<BGCOLOR= "#hexvalue">	This tag specifies the background color for a particular space. When used in the body tag = <BODY BGCOLOR ="#CFCFCF"> it renders the whole page the color specified. It can also be used as an attribute tag for any of the table tags.
	Here "hexvalue" is the six-character combination of letters and numbers that a browser reads as a color. For example, BGCOLOR="#FFFFFF" tells the browser the color is white. Most browsers also support the option BGCOLOR="white", but hexadecimal colors are much more accurate across platforms and browsers.

HTML Basics

Building on the tag overview in the previous tables, the following sections review some of the HTML formats and tricks that you'll need to know to work with the book's later material.

Tables

Tables enable you to visually organize data. The contents of a table are contained within two table tags and broken out by horizontal rows. Each row is comprised of table cells.

Example   A basic table

```
<TABLE>
<TR>
<TT>This is the title</TT>
<TD>Row 1, cell 1</TD>
<TD>Row 1, cell 2</TD>
</TR>
```

continues

continued

```
<TR>
<TD>Row 2, cell 1</TD>
<TD>Row 2, cell 2</TD>
</TR>
</TABLE>
```

The preceding code is illustrated in figure 2.2.

Figure 2.2

A basic HTML table. Remember that when you write HTML for a table, the cells are arranged horizontally, not vertically.

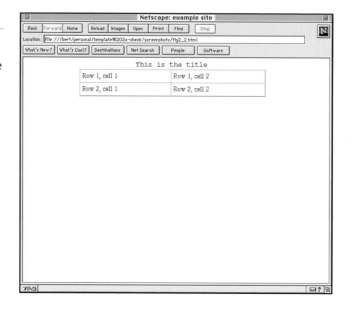

Table Formatting Basics

The tags covered in the following sections don't alter the structural organization of the table contents, but can alter the appearance of the table.

You might want to use tables to achieve an exact layout. Table alignment tags can line text and images up along vertical and horizontal axes and can help you create strong eyelines within a web page. Tables can also control spacing of page elements with a finer degree of control than regular markup tags. You can, for example, table three horizontal elements and specify cellspacing for them. A recent addition to the table's bag of layout tricks is the bgcolor tag—you can now use color to code the content of your table cells, emphasize information on a page, or add a no-gif color punch to your page.

NOTE

Using tables to achieve specific layout effects is a smart way to use HTML, but it's not one that reflects the structural integrity of the language. HTML purists would argue that you should only use tables if your information is meant to be organized as such. If you're designing a site that tries to use HTML in a strictly functional sense, tables will not solve any of your layout dilemmas. In addition, tables only work on browsers that support HTML 2.0 or better. That's not a significant percentage anymore, but it's still something you might want to consider.

Now that you've learned about the various uses of table tags and the attendant usability issues, the following sections will review the table tags and all their properties so that you can see how they work.

<TABLE BORDER>

This tag sets the border of your table to zero. This is handy when you want to use a table as a layout device—organizing text items at a set distance from each other—without a distracting border (see figures 2.3 and 2.4).

Figure 2.3

Table with border set to 5.

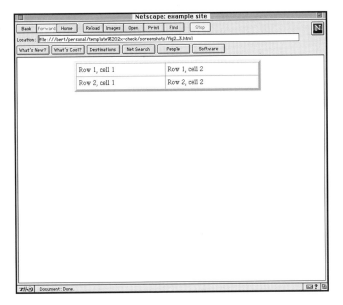

Figure 2.4

Table with border set to 0.

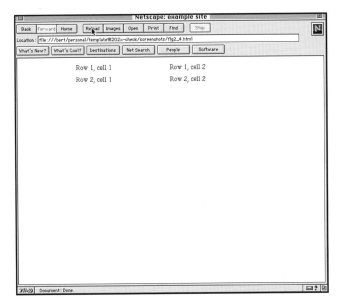

The border tag is also a good way to test how the elements in your table relate to each other—build a table with the BORDER = 1, then set it to zero when the site goes live.

<TABLE CELLSPACING>

The cellspacing tag determines the distance, in pixels, that individual cells will be from each other. This distance affects all four directions (left, right, top, and bottom). Cellspacing is a good way to control the distance that different elements in a table will have from each other. If you're using a table to push graphic images flush to each other within a precise space, <TABLE CELLPADDING = 0> is a great way to accomplish this (see fig. 2.5).

Figure 2.5

Using cellspacing to control the distance that table elements lay in relation to one another.

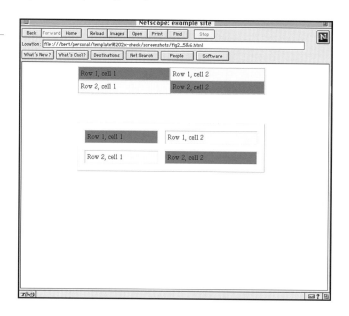

If you're trying to create maximum whitespace between different elements in a table, <TABLE CELLSPACING = 12> would work (see fig. 2.6).

<TABLE CELLPADDING>

Cell padding affects the spatial placement of the table contents. The setting, CELLPADDING = 0, visually tightens the space between the contents of the cell and the cell edges; the setting, CELLPADDING = 5, surrounds the table cell contents with 5 pixels of space on every side. Figure 2.6 shows examples of table contents with and without cellpadding.

Figure 2.6

The top table has a border of 1 and no cellspacing; the bottom table has a border of 1 and CELLSPACING = 12.

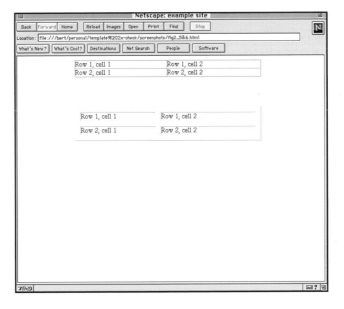

Figure 2.7

The top table has a border of 1 and no cellpadding; the bottom table has a border of 1 and CELLPADDING = 12.

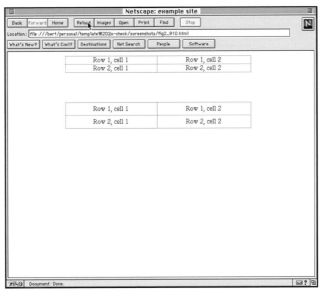

Cellpadding is best used to fine-tune the way elements sit within a table cell. If you're floating a red square within a white-background table, and you want it to appear flush to a blue square, you'll want to code <CELLPADDING = 0> to make sure the browser sets the edges of the table cell as close to the content as possible. If you'd like to align the elements, but don't care beyond that, you can either ignore the cellpadding tag or set it to 1.

Cellspacing Versus Cellpadding

The <TABLE CELLSPACING> and <TABLE CELLPADDING> tags are about space—the question is where the space goes. In cellspacing, the pixels surround each cell as shown in figure 2.8.

Figure 2.8

The top table has a border of 1 and no cellpadding; the bottom table has a border of 1 and CELLPADDING = 5.

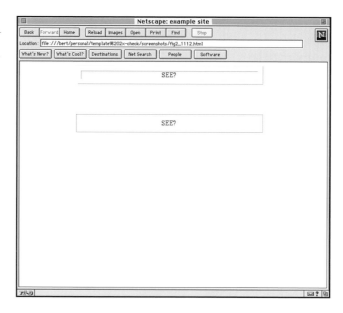

The advantage to using cellspacing is an evenly distributed spacing across the entire table. If the purpose of your table is to align elements, the cellspacing tag is a good tag to use. The disadvantage is that you can't set cellspacing row by row, so you must decide if all the table elements are going to be flush to each other, or far away from each other.

The advantage to using cellpadding is a visual cushion of space around elements within the table. For text-intensive tables, this provides the eye with a much-needed break, and enables the user to focus on individual elements. The disadvantage is that space is considered part of the cell contents, consequently increasing the length and width of the table cell and possibly throwing off the table proportions.

NOTE Two properties about the cellspacing and cellpadding tags that you should remember are: if the tag is not specified, the browser will assume a default value of 1, and remember that these elements are all attached to the table tag—and you can specify more than one element at a time.

If you look at the following example, you'll see that three of the table's layout features have been specified: cell spacing (pixels of space around the table), cell padding (pixels of space around the inside of each table cell), and table border.

```
<TABLE BORDER = 0 CELLPADDING = 5 CELLSPACING = 5>
```

Aligning Table Contents

You already know that you can use tables to control the physical placement of page elements—or at least their physical placement relative to each other. The tags discussed in the following sections control where text and graphic elements are placed within table rows and table cells. These tags can be used to create a strong horizontal eyeline across table cells, or a strong vertical margin along the side of a table (see fig. 2.9).

Figure 2.9

Arranging table cells with BORDER = 0, CELLSPACING = 5, and CELLPADDING = 5 to create the illusion of floating elements.

These tags exist as layout tags, not structural tags, so the issue of misappropriating the tags for layout purposes is moot. Be warned, however, that these tags must be used consistently or you'll get some odd-looking layouts. Any tag that doesn't have a vertical or horizontal alignment defaults to a center-center placement. This doesn't sound bad until you notice that table cell size correlates to the largest cell in the row and the column—one word floating in the center of the table cell can disrupt a layout. The tags in the following sections should be used to place table cell contents as precisely as possible in relation to each other.

<TR VALIGN>

The <TR VALIGN> tag aligns the contents of a row of table cells along a vertical axis—top, middle, or bottom. Figures 2.10, 2.11, and 2.12 illustrate top, middle, and bottom aligned tables, respectively. The source code for each table is included for posterity.

```
<TR VALIGN = top>
<TD>qwerty</TD>
<TD>asdfghjkl</TD>
<TD>zxc</TD>
</TR>

<TR VALIGN = middle>
<TD>qwerty</TD>
<TD>asdfghjkl</TD>
<TD>zxc</TD>
</TR>
```

```
<TR VALIGN = bottom >
<TD>qwerty</TD>
<TD>asdfghjkl</TD>
<TD>zxc</TD>
</TR>
```

Figure 2.10

A table with vertical alignment set to the top of the table. The effect is especially apparent in Row 1, cell 2.

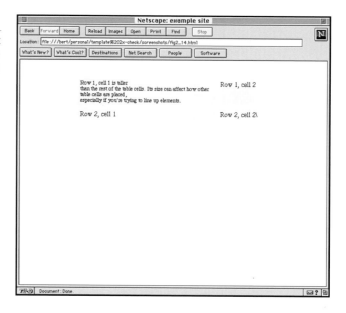

Figure 2.11

A table with vertical alignment set to the middle of the table. The effect is especially apparent in Row 1, cell 2.

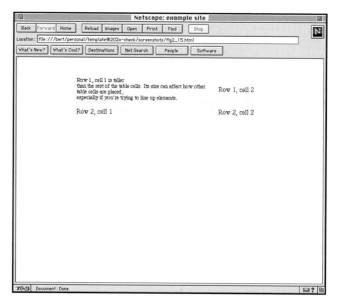

<TD VALIGN>

The <TD VALIGN> tag performs the same functions as the <TR VALIGN> tag, except on a cell-by-cell basis. A <TR VALIGN> tag overrides a <TD VALIGN> tag (row over cell).

Figure 2.12

A table with vertical alignment set to the bottom of the table. The effect is especially apparent in Row 1, cell 2.

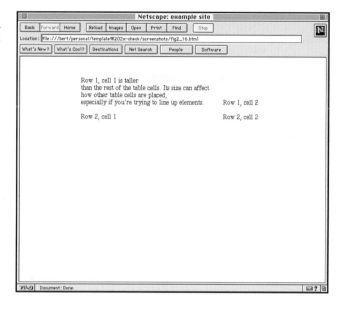

<TR HALIGN>

The <TR HALIGN> tag aligns the contents of a row of table cells along a horizontal axis—left, middle, or right. The <TR HALIGN> tag affects where table cell contents lay relative to the left or right table cell edges. Figures 2.13, 2.14, and 2.15 illustrate left, middle, and right-aligned tables, respectively. The source code for each table is included for posterity.

Figure 2.13

A table with horizontal alignment set to the left. The effect is especially apparent in Row 1, cell 2.

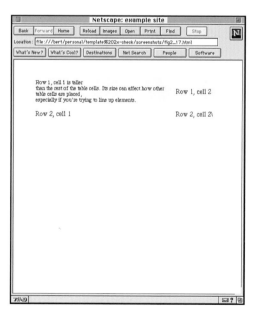

```
<TR HALIGN = left>
<TD>qwerty</TD>
<TD>asdfghjkl</TD>
<TD>zxc</TD>
</TR>

<TR HALIGN = middle>
<TD>qwerty</TD>
<TD>asdfghjkl</TD>
<TD>zxc</TD>
</TR>
<TR HALIGN = right>
<TD>qwerty</TD>
<TD>asdfghjkl</TD>
<TD>zxc</TD>
</TR>
```

Figure 2.14

A table with horizontal alignment set to the middle. The effect is especially apparent in Row 1, cell 2.

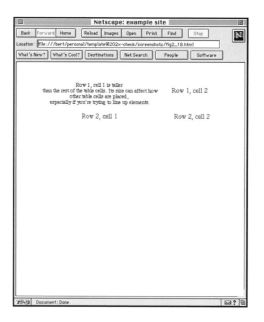

<TD HALIGN>

The <TD HALIGN> tag performs the same functions as the <TR HALIGN> tag, except on a cell-by-cell basis. A <TR HALIGN > tag overrides a <TD HALIGN > tag (row over cell).

Figure 2.15

A table with horizontal alignment set to the right. The effect is especially apparent in Row 1, cell 2.

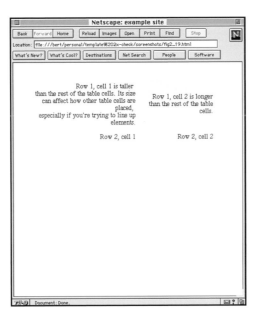

<COLSPAN>

The <COLSPAN> tag extends a table cell over more than one column over a horizontal row of cells. Be aware that this tag does not change the number of table cells in a given row. If you're going to extend a cell across two columns, subtract the cell that your expanding piece is taking over.

You might use this tag for formatting if you're inserting a particularly long graphic or text chunk and you're trying to maintain a strict layout. Remember that table cells automatically resize to fit the biggest cell in the row and in the column. Extending a table cell across two rows enables you to place items within a table that are proportionally taller than their counterparts. Extending a table cell across two columns allows you to place wider table objects. The long table cell takes up the space that two cells would normally occupy, resulting in a table row with fewer cells as shown in figure 2.16. You can use the tags in the following source code to vary the sizes and shapes of your table cells—thus enabling you to use a table to layout several different sized items.

```
<TABLE>
    <TR>
    <TD COLSPAN = 2>This covers all items in these two colmuns in the rows
    ➡below</TD>

    <TD>Other cell
    </TD>
    </TR>
    <TR>
    <TD>Other cell
    </TD>
```

```
<TD>Other cell
</TD>
<TD>Other cell
</TD>
</TR>
</TABLE>
```

Figure 2.16

A table with one cell set to COLSPAN = 2.

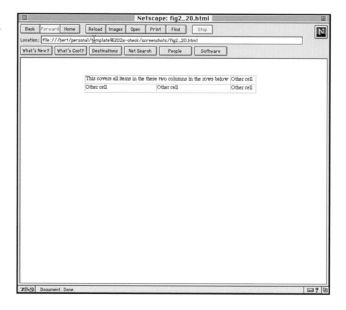

<ROWSPAN>

The <ROWSPAN> tag extends a table cell over more than one row. Be aware that this tag does not change the number of table cells in a given row; it just enables two or more cells to merge on a vertical axis.

You might use this tag as demonstrated in the source code and resulting figure 2.17 to create subheadings within a table (a structural use), or to control the spatial arrangement of elements within a table (a formatting use).

```
<TABLE>
<TR>
<TD>content</TD>
<TD>content</TD>
<TD>content</TD>
</TR>
<TR>
<TD ROWSPAN = 2>All four of these cells are related because I say so</TD>
<TD>content</TD>
```

```
                <TD>content</TD>

            </TR>

            <TR>

                <TD>content</TD>

                <TD>content</tD>

            </TR>

        </TABLE>
```

Figure 2.17

Table with a cell with
ROWSPAN = 2. Rowspan cells
display from the top down.

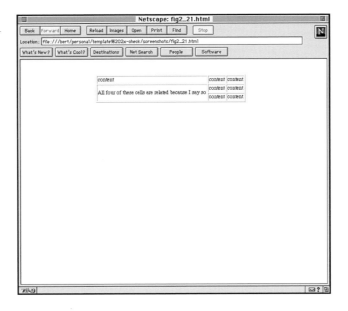

Embedding Tables

Writing HTML so that one table of data appears within another isn't something that many structural HTML purists approve. Designers argue that this method provides a finer degree of control over the precise line-up of elements in a document.

The principle item in embedding tables is simple to remember: your embedded table equals the contents of one table cell. The actual HTML is a little more daunting because it requires you to pay strict attention to which <TD> and <TR> you just closed, and to which table they belong. Embedding tables is a good way to represent complex groups of data in relation to one another, or to tightly control the spatial relationship between different elements on a page. You might find that indenting different levels of structural HTML—in the following source code and figure 2.18, the main table and the data within it—helps to visually separate all the parts.

```
        <TABLE>

            <TR>

            <TD>content</TD>

            <TD>content</TD>

            <TD>content</TD>
```

```
        </TR>
        <TR>
        <TD>content</TD>
        <TD>
            <TABLE>
                <TR>
                <TD>content</TD>
                <TD>content</TD>
                </TR>
            </TABLE>
        </TD>
        <TD>content</TD>
        </TR>
    </TABLE>
```

Figure 2.18

Embedding a two cell table inside a table cell in a larger table.

Color

Color adds a fresh and dynamic visual aspect to web pages: it can enliven blocks of text, provide a visual hierarchy for users, and give the web site a distinctive look. The CD-ROM fully illustrates the following examples, so you may want to reference as you read this section. Figure 2.19 demonstrates how color disntinguishes between different elements on a web site.

Color can also ruin a web site if it's not used carefully. Think about web sites where the text is nearly indistinguishable from the background color or stands out so violently your eyeballs begin to vibrate. Another abuse of color occurs in web sites where so many colors are used that you're not sure where to look first.

Figure 2.19

Using color wisely as a visual reinforcement of content.

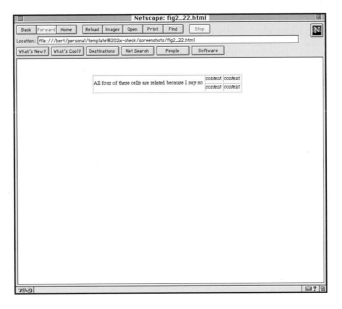

In figure 2.20, the designer has added a lot of colors just for the sake of adding various colors. Not only aren't there any clear correlations between the colors and the information tied into them, so many colors appear that it is hard to find one clear focal point for the page.

Figure 2.20

A really bad use of table cell color that fails to establish a relationship between content and color.

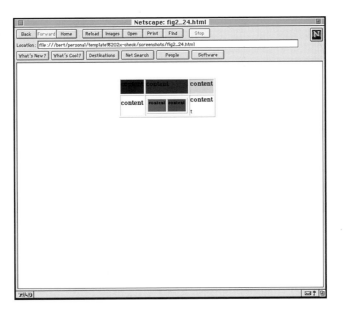

Successful use of color relies on a few basic rules:

❖ **Use Color as an Information Cue:** Make the "About This Web Site" pages yellow and the "What's New" pages blue—your readers will be able to assess contents with these visual cues.

❖ **Use Color to Provide Visual Cohesion Across the Site:** This doesn't mean that you have to stick with the same two colors on every page in the site—just utilize color in the same way throughout. If your readers know that vital information will always be colorfully contrasted against background information, this interface detail will provide a sense of familiarity and comfort—something a good interface should always do.

❖ **Use Color as an Enhancement, not a Principal Building Block:** Because few guarantees of consistency exist in equipment or software across the web, any color-based items are going to have to be built in a way that works well within the tools used to view the web site, and in a way that does not detract from or clash with the content of the web site.

Visual considerations are only some of the ponderables when you begin thinking about using color; there are also technical considerations. Think about the variety of browsers and platforms your users may be using. What appears to be a delicate, pale peach background on your monitor could show up an orange-brown on someone else's screen. If you're going to use a palette of colors to establish a distinctive look and feel for your site, you will want to dither them down to the lowest possible value to ensure the most consistency across your audience.

Also remember that text users or people with grayscale screens won't be able to see the colors. If you're relying on the colors in your web site to act as navigational devices, or a way of distinguishing different levels of content, you may want to provide alternative methods of annotating content.

The following sections illustrate a few methods to enliven web pages after you've determined how to best use color to enhance your web site.

Background Colors Versus Background Graphics

When Netscape 1.1 was released, the effect on the web was analogous to Dorothy's landing in Oz—a black-and-white world exploded in color. That browser was the first to include the tags that would enable web page builders to break free of the gray background.

Adding a background color to a web page is easy. Find the hex value of the color you want, and write it in the body tag:

```
<BODY BGCOLOR = "#FFFFFF">
```

NOTE

For those of you asking what a *hex value* is, computers recognize hexadecimal values for some types of data. In this case, your browser recognizes it and produces a color in response. Microsoft Internet Explorer also recognizes: black, maroon, green, olive, gray, navy, purple, teal, silver, red, lime, yellow, blue, fuchsia, aqua, and white as color tags, but a hex number guarantees a finer degree of control over the end result.

You can determine the hex value of a given color in a few ways: by visiting a web site, picking a color you like, and finding out the corresponding hex value, or by converting the RGB color value to hex (the web site BeachRat— `http://www.novalink.com/pei/hex/hex.html`— does a great job).

Or, you can forgo adding a <BGCOLOR> tag and add a background image. The HTML for this is:

```
<BODY BACKGROUND = "foo.gif">
```

Just remember: your web site should still work for a user who has the images turned off, and you want your images to be as lightweight as possible so that it doesn't delay downloading the web page.

Coloring Text

Adding color to blocks of text can be accomplished in several ways, as discussed in the next couple of examples.

You can alter all the text in a page by writing a text color tag within the body tag. Like background colors, the value for text colors is usually a hex value, and it looks like this:

```
<BODY TEXT = "#000000">
```

In addition, you can also add color to blocks of text via links. This is a great way to provide readers with a visual cue of where they've visited and where they haven't. Hyperlinks should always be distinguishable from regular text. Link color tags are also added within the body tags, and break down like this:

- ❖ **link = "#FF0000":** for links you haven't visited yet
- ❖ **vlink = "#0000FF":** for links you have visited
- ❖ **alink = "#00FF00":** this color flashes as the user clicks on the link

In action, the tag for adding background and text color would look like this:

```
<BODY BGCOLOR = "#FFFFFF" LINK = "#FF0000" VLINK = "#0000FF" TEXT = "#000000">
```

The output of this tag is illustrated in figure 2.21:

Figure 2.21

Using color to begin and end a hyperlink (red text) within the body text (black text).

You can also forgo the body text tag, and emphasize chunks of text with different colors as shown in the following source code and figure 2.22:

```
<FONT COLOR="#3C3CD3" SIZE=7><B>Heading</B></FONT><P>

<FONT COLOR= "#FF0000" SIZE=5>Another stylistic quirk</FONT><P>

<FONT SIZE="3"><B>text here is a default color, usually black</B></FONT>
```

Figure 2.22

Emphasizing text with color
and font size.

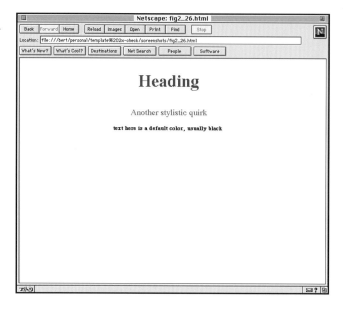

Note the use of the <FONT> tag—a recent addition to HTML. The <FONT> tag, which you'll read about in a few more paragraphs, is another functional tag. It works well on an item-by-item basis, as opposed to the <BODY TEXT> tag, which works across the page.

Coloring Table Cells

Another recent addition to HTML is the capability to add color to a limited element within an HTML document—the table cell. By adding the <COLOR = "#6C6C6C"> to any element in a table, you can control the color of parts of the table. A few pointers:

❖ You can still have a body background tag and table background color tags.

❖ Adding the color tag to the table <TABLE BGCOLOR = "#55F55F"> colors the whole table.

❖ Adding the color tag to the row <TR BGCOLOR ="#55F55F"> colors a table row.

❖ Adding the color tag to the table cell <TD BGCOLOR ="#55F55F"> colors a table cell.

❖ You may want to make sure the design you have works across browsers that don't support HTML 3.2 (anything below Netscape 3.0/MSIE 3.0).

In figure 2.23, the table shows two different uses of the <BGCOLOR> tag. The first row has a <TR BGCOLOR> tag, and the second has three individual <TD BGCOLOR> tags.

Figure 2.23

Distinguishing table elements with color.

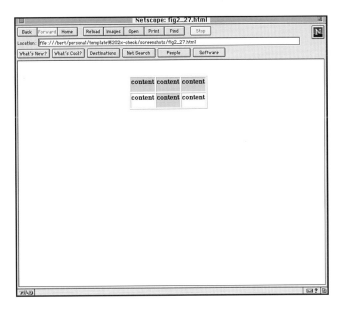

Text

There are two schools of thought about mixing and matching text tags—one advocates sticking to structural tags, and the other embraces formatting tags (this surprises you?).

Both schools are correct, to a point. Text size can be used to establish a hierarchy of information, a visual inverted pyramid of most-important to least-important. Different *fonts*, however, can provide cues as to which level of information an item belongs.

A text outline using structural tags, for example, would look like this:

```
<H1>I. Kingdom: Animalia</H1><BR>

<H2>A. Phylum: Chordata</H2><BR>

<H3>1. Class: Mammalia</H3><BR>

<H4>a. Order: Primates</H4><BR>

<P>

<H1>I. Kingdom: Protista</H1><BR>

<H2>A.  Phylum: Archaebacteria</H2></BR>

<P>
```

Figure 2.24 illustrates the preceding source code.

It's functional, but perhaps not the most visually exciting thing you could do with the information. The example that follows varies the font face and font sizes to indicate different categories in the information structure.

Figure 2.24

Using font sizes to denote an information hierarchy. This is functional, but not very attractive.

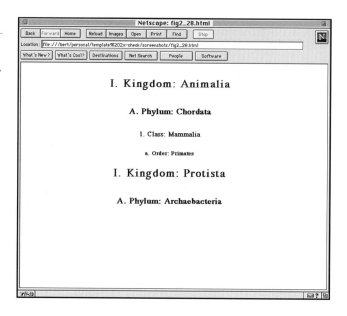

```
<FONT FACE = "arial, helvetica" size = +5>Kingdom: Animalia</FONT><P>
<FONT SIZE = +3>A. Phylum: Chordata</FONT><BR>
<FONT SIZE = +2>1. Class: Mammalia</FONT><BR>
<FONT SIZE = +1>a. Order: Primates</FONT><BR>
<P>
<FONT FACE = "arial, helvetica" size = +5>I. Kingdom: Protista</FONT><P>
<FONT SIZE = +3>A.  Phylum: Archaebacteria</FONT><BR>
<P>
```

Figure 2.25 illustrates the preceding source code.

Figure 2.25

Using font faces and sizes to denote an information hierarchy.

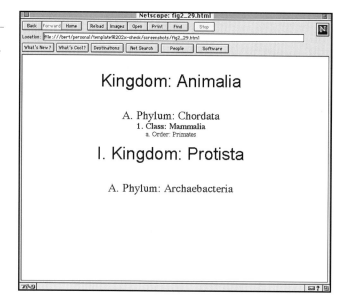

Introducing different fonts is a great way to attractively represent lots of information, but be sure to limit your fonts to a serif and a sans serif, and to have a corresponding informational function. In other words, don't introduce different font faces just for the heck of it—have it mean something.

Regarding size, you can always write <FONT SIZE = "–7 – +7> </FONT> and the text within the tags will scale to the browser's values for that font size as shown in the following examples:

```
<FONT SIZE = -1> This is good for footnotes</FONT>

<FONT SIZE = +4> This is good for page headlines</FONT>
```

Regarding font face, all fonts fall into one of two categories—serif or sans serif. The term *serif* refers to the extensions on open or finishing strokes as shown in the following font examples:

Times   Helvetica

Notice how the Times font—a serif font—has little "feet" on the ends of the letter lines, while the Helvetica font ends without any extensions.

You can use fonts as a visual code for information. For example, a sans serif font for headings and captions, a serif font for contents, or as a way of establishing look and feel across the web site. An early way of using fonts to set up look and feel was to use the structural tag <TT></TT> to change the text from the browser default to the browser true type. In most browsers, <TT></TT> looks like Courier text.

So, considering the two traits just discussed—size and font face—plus color, you can make text a vital design component in your web site.

Figures 2.26 and 2.27 each illustrate different points. Figure 2.26 shows how colored text can accent a web page and add visual interest. Figure 2.27 shows how font faces can add a visual lexicon for the information in a web page.

Figure 2.26

Using color to differentiate chunks of information within a page. Color indicates new sections; the font face stays constant.

Figure 2.27

Using font faces to differentiate chunks of information within a page. The font faces indicate new sections; the color stays constant.

The <FONT> tag is another tag where you can keep adding attributes to specify what the element should look like as shown in the following example:

```
<FONT FACE= "helvetica, arial" COLOR = "#FF0000" SIZE = +6>Bold Heading</FONT>
```

Forms

This is the first interactive aspect of web site treated in this chapter. Forms serve a variety of purposes on a web site—providing you with a means to collect data, or providing users the chance to give you feedback. This chapter won't go into the mechanics of how a form works, but focuses on the information-containing elements of form design.

The elements of a form are shown in the following source code and in figure 2.28.

```
<FORM ACTION="local/cgi-bin/comments.pl" METHOD="POST<P>
What is your email address?
<INPUT TYPE="text" NAME="email" VALUE="" SIZE=42 MAXLENGTH=50>
<P>
Write your comments:
<INPUT TYPE="text" TEXTAREA ROWS=15 NAME="feedback" COLS=40 WRAP=Physical>
</TEXTAREA>
<P>
<INPUT TYPE=Submit VALUE="Done"></FORM>
```

Figure 2.28

A basic web form with a comment area and a submit button.

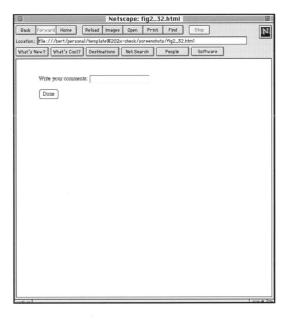

The form is contained within the tags <FORM></FORM>. The ACTION = is an element of the form tag telling the web site server which script is going to handle incoming data ("local/cgi-bin/comments.pl") and by what method the data will be moving from user to web server (METHOD = post). User input is noted with <INPUT> tags—what type of input depends on the attributes discussed in the following sections.

Form Elements to Play With

Four types of form tags to play with when dealing with forms are:

- ❖ <SELECT>
- ❖ </SELECT>
- ❖ <OPTION>
- ❖ <INPUT>

The first two tags go together—<SELECT></SELECT>—and provide a menu of choices for your users. Pull-down menus are just a string of options (noted as <OPTION>) within select tags, such as the following:

```
<FORM>
<SELECT>
<OPTION>The top line is a default
<OPTION>Each item in the select menu
<OPTION>has its own option entry.
<OPTION>Notice option has no closing tags
</SELECT>
</FORM>
```

Figure 2.29 illustrates the preceding source code.

Figure 2.29

A selected pull-down menu.

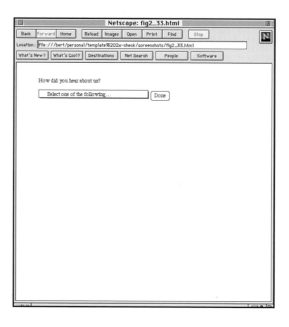

A pull-down menu is best used as a space-saving navigational device. They can also be used to include lengthy lists within an order form or other interactive page—again, this saves space and is easily updated or pared.

The <INPUT> tag notifies the browser that a form option is running; which option you want to employ is specified as part of the tag, as type = .

❖ **<INPUT TYPE = checkbox>:** This tag creates a standard check box option. This option is a good choice if you want your user to select more than one item in an array of choices.

Some sites use form conventions in lieu of setting up a sidebar on a web page. The specifics won't be touched upon here, but if you want to experiment with this, the following tips may help.

❖ Every <FORM> tag cues a new paragraph, so if you want to embed any type of form within a body of text, type <FORM>, add the content, then insert the form tags. Don't forget to close the paragraph with a </FORM> tag.

❖ You can insert other format-based tags after an <INPUT> tag, thus enabling you to alter the font facing, size, weight, or characteristic of the option you're presenting to your viewer. You can also apply conventional text-layout tags.

Advantages of Frames

The HTML addition of frames pushes web sites out of flat-page model and accentuates the possibilities of hyperlinking text. A web page comprised of two or more frames combines two documents and introduces a variety of new navigational paths and ways of looking at the data. Figure 2.30 symbolically illustrates the possible paths a user can take from just one hyperlink in just one frame.

Figure 2.30

A schema that demonstrates how to target links to open new pages in a specific frame. The black squares illustrate link targeting: the page loads in the black square even if the hyperlink that references it lives in another frame (colored square) on the web site.

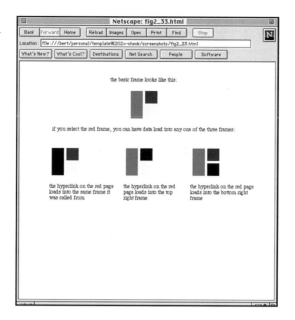

Although framed content can be dynamic and completely separate from other framed parts of a web page, a framed web page can also provide a constant interface feature if one part of the document acts as a navigational device or other user feature.

The following section provides source code and explanation on how a framed document works.

Basic Frames Document/Frame Tags

The code for a basic framed document looks like this:

```
<HTML>
<HEAD>
<TITLE>Frames example</TITLE>
<FRAMESET COLS = 25%, 75%>
<FRAMESRC = "leftframe.html" NAME = "left">
<FRAME SRC = "rightframe.html" NAME= "right">
</FRAMESET>
</HEAD>
</HTML>
```

The different parts of a framed document are illustrated in figure 2.31 and in the text that follows the figure.

The <FRAMESET> tags signal the beginning and the end of the frames document. These replace the <BODY> tags you would use to indicate content that is to be loaded into the browser window.

Figure 2.31

A very basic example of
frames. Keep in mind that
each frame loads a separate
HTML file.

The <FRAMESET COLS = 25%, 75%> set up the proportion of the framed parts to each other.
You can write these values as percentages of total browser width, or if one frame is based on an
exact measure, by pixels, like this <FRAMESET COLS = 100, *>. The asterisk allows for the other
part of the framed document to adjust to the remainder of the browser window. Note also that
the tag says <FRAMESET COLS>—thus denoting a vertical division. The <FRAMESET ROWS = >
tag sets the frame horizontally across the browser window.

The <FRAMESRC> tags call the separate HTML files that appear in each frame—one file per
frame. In essence, the framed document is three separate files: two content files (leftframe.html
and rightframe.html) and one uberfile that pulls them into position. Looking at the <FRAMESRC>
tags—the browser always reads these left to right—the following example illustrates this by naming
the documents "left" and "right." The name has nothing to do with where the frame is placed:

```
<HTML>

<FRAMESET ROWS ="25%,75%">

<FRAME SRC ="red.html" name=" red ">

    <FRAMESET COLS="200,*">

    <FRAME SRC="blue.html" name="blue">

    <FRAME SRC="cyellowy.html" name="yellow">

    </FRAMESET>

</FRAMESET>

</HTML>
```

NOTE

Regardless of the names, the frames still load in the specified order.

Figure 2.32 illustrates how you can keep adding frames and pulling more pages into your web layout.

Figure 2.32

Using frames to maintain a narrative indicated in the black squares.

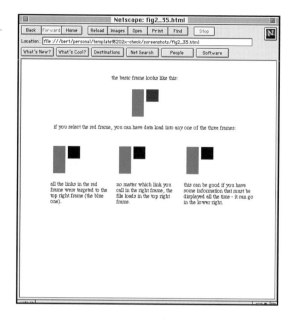

It is also possible to write so that more than one frame is on a screen. The code breaks down like this:

- ❖ **<FRAMESET ROWS = 25%, 75%>:** Sets up two separate parts of the document.
- ❖ **<FRAMESRC = "larry.html" NAME = "larry">:** Fills the 25 percent space.
- ❖ **<FRAMSET COLS = "200, *">:** The beginning of the code that fills up the 75 percent space. This cues the browser to *further* divide this space into a 200 pixel area and a variable area.
  - ◆ <FRAME SRC="moe.html" NAME="moe">
  - ◆ <FRAME SRC="curly.html" NAME="curly">
- ❖ **</FRAMESET>:** Finishes up the code for the 75 percent part of the browser.
- ❖ **</FRAMESET>:** Indicates the entire frames document is done.

You can fine-tune the appearance of your frames by incorporating the following tags:

- ❖ **<FRAMESET BORDER = 0>:** This leaves no discernible border between your frames. It's good for creating a seamless, truly hyperlinking page—provided at least one of the frames is precisely sized to prevent sloppy user navigation on the page.
- ❖ **<FRAMESRC= "" MARGINHEIGHT = x>:** This tag enables you to set up a horizontal margin within your frame. You could use it to provide a cushion of space on the top and bottom of the frame.
- ❖ **<FRAMESRC= "" MARGINWIDTH = x>:** This tag enables you to set up a vertical margin within your frame. You could use it to provide a cushion of space on the left and right of the frame.
- ❖ **<FRAMESRC = "" SCROLLING = AUTO>:** This tells the browser to automatically add scrolling if the frame and browser window size do not allow all the frame's content to be displayed at once.

❖ **<FRAMESRC = "" SCROLLING = no>:** You can guarantee that the same content within a frame will always be displayed—no scrolling up, down, left, or right—just by removing the scrolling option. This is not a tag that wins a lot of friends in usability circles, but can be used for design if the presentation is absolutely dependent on a certain frame layout.

Providing a Non-Frames Alternative

Not all browsers support frames—especially text-based browsers. It's a good usability trait to provide a non-frames alternative, and it's possible to do so within the same .html file as your frames document.

The structure for the document is similar to:

```
<HTML>
<FRAMESET 25%, 75%>
<FRAMESRC = "left.html " NAME = "left">
<FRAMESRC = "right.html" NAME = "right">
</FRAMESET>
<NOFRAMES>
<BODY>
<--insert alternative content here-->
</BODY>
</NOFRAMES>
</HTML>
```

So, frames content is always contained in <FRAMESET> tags. Non-frames content is cued by the <NOFRAMES> tag, and contained in typical <BODY> tags. The no-frames alternative ends with the </NOFRAMES> tag, and both "documents" end with the closing <HTML> tag.

Different Frame Layouts

As the diagram with the different colored blocks demonstrated, the variety of navigational paths your user has when clicking on links within frames documents is much greater than a typical one-file-per-window web site. This can be good if you're using your web site as a performance art piece, and the experience is deliberately nonlinear. One of the main features about frames that makes them attractive to web designers, however, is that one can use one part of a frame as a static navigational device while content changes within the other part of the frame.

How do you do this? Start with opening a new file within a frame.

Returning to the document:

```
<HTML>
<FRAMESET 25%, 75%>
<FRAMESRC = "left.html" NAME = "left">
<FRAMESRC = "right.html" NAME = "right">
```

POSSIBLE USES OF FRAMES

```
</FRAMESET>
</HTML>
```

Assume that hyperlinks are somewhere in the document left.html. If you want to open one of these hyperlinks in the frame portion previously occupied by right.html, you need to follow these steps:

1. Open the left.html source code, because that's where the link in question lives.
2. Take a look at the <A HREF> for the link
3. Include the following tag:
   <A HREF= "newfile.html" TARGET = "right">.
   This tells the browser to load newfile.html into the part of the frame named "right."

Remember in the <FRAMESRC> tag, there are two parts: the name of file providing source code for the frame, and the name of the frame itself.

If you want the link within your frame source code to bring up a new and different window (to not load into the frames page), then go to the frame source code, identify the hyperlink you want, and where you would enter your target value, type "TARGET = "_top".

This cues the browser to leave the framed document completely and instructs the browser to open a new web page.

Text Browser Work-Arounds

If your code is built close to W3 standards, the pages should degrade smoothly across all sorts of browsers. Degrading HTML doesn't mean making fun of your markup—it means HTML that can preserve its structure and layout across older browsers and lower-end machines and monitors. Good HTML degrades smoothly, so someone viewing your web page in Lynx, or with the images off can still understand what's on each web page and interact with it.

Preserving a textual skeleton throughout a web site is getting increasingly difficult. Web sites are becoming increasingly graphically oriented, and many interface features are now exclusively graphic. Image maps are a good example of this. You'll have to stay abreast of the latest web trends (graphics or no), but you can still work on making your web site widely accessible by doing one or more of the following:

❖ **Using Alt Tags Behind your Graphics:** People cruising without the images turned on are more likely to download the image if they know what the image is and how it links to the site. It's not necessary to write an alt tag paragraph—a short and accurate description, like "annual report graphic," is much more helpful than "—."

❖ **Providing Text Alternatives:** An image map can be a visually elegant and concise representation of a complex information hierarchy, but it's useless if someone can't or won't view it. A small, unobtrusive bar of hyperlinks reinforces the navigation tools on the page and provides a means of interacting for the image-challenged.

❖ **Sticking to Structural HTML:** The single-pixel-gif-as-text leading trick looks great on fully loaded browsers, but what about text-only browsers or images-off? Not everyone has instant access to a T1 and a 19-inch screen. Design your HTML so that it presents the information as attractively as possible, not so that it manages to fit the information on the page after the design is settled.

Conditional HTML

By-the-book use of HTML is the most basic way to guarantee that an audience with a wide range of browsers, computer platforms, and connection speeds can see your site. Another way is to send back web pages targeted toward their browser or platform. You can do this by following two steps:

1. Figure out what environmental variables you will need to detect.
2. Write an if-then in your HTML that will enable the server to send the correct HTML to the visiting browser.

An environmental variable is a piece of information passed from the client to the server. When a user (client) clicks on a link calling up your web page (server), s/he passes along a lot of useful information. This useful information includes the type of browser software the client has, what machine the client is coming from, what domain the client is coming from, and what sort of connection protocol the client is using.

You can take this information and serve HTML that depends on one of the variables in response. If, for example, you want to serve a page with frames, but would like to provide a non-frames alternative, you could write conditional HTML that says "if supports=frames"—insert the frames HTML—"else"—insert the non-frames HTML.

It's not as easy as writing an if-then statement, however—you will need to work with your server administrator to write a script that processes the environmental variables and serves the HTML. Your job is to provide the cue to the server.

Graphics

The majority of this book will concentrate on building smart HTML, but images are a vibrant part of web sites too. You might be called on to create or modify graphics. For a thorough and expert primer on creating great web graphics, I recommend that you read Lynda Weinman's book, *Designing Web Graphics*. This chapter focuses on the very basics for graphics legibility—size and transparency.

Size

Graphic size can be translated two ways: the length and height of the graphic, and the size of the file. Knowing and manipulating size in both senses of the word is important. If you're using tables to line up different page elements, knowing the graphic dimension can help you lay out the table. If you're concerned about the total page file size and its download time, optimizing the graphics file size can cut time off the download.

Unfortunately, the best graphics manipulation tools are not free. Adobe Photoshop is a great all-purpose graphics application; Aldus Illustrator is another good all-purpose package; and DeBabelizer is a powerful tool to have in your graphics toolkit.

A number of good free or shareware programs are out on the Net as well. Two of my favorites are Jpeg View and GifBuilder. Jpeg View can't create graphics, but it's a handy tool for checking file size and graphic dimensions, and it's a quick means of scaling a picture up or down.

GifBuilder does precisely what its name implies: it takes a series of gifs and strings them together to make an animated gif. Be very, very careful if using this tool! Animation can be eyecatching, quirky, or even purposeful, but infinitely looping animation can quickly move from purposeful to irritating.

The temptation to loop graphics notwithstanding, GifBuilder is also a good tool for moderating animation speed, reducing the size of the graphic, and pulling static images from an animated file.

Transparency

When background colors and patterns were introduced to web page design, web site builders eagerly wrote tags like "BGCOLOR="#FFFFFF", hit reload, and gasped in horror as they realized all their graphics had been created with gray background canvases. The up and down arrows that used to float on the page were now ugly gray splotches, the headline graphic a clunky box of text.

Recreating all the graphics was time-consuming, and presented a design issue: What did one do about users who would still be viewing pages with a browser that did not support background colors? The answer: don't re-create the entire graphic, but make the background of the graphic "transparent." This means the graphic will still appear to "float" on the background of your (or the user's) choice.

Transparent graphics are now a norm in web design. For creating them, nothing beats Photoshop or DeBabelizer, but you can still work transparency wonders with freeware. Transparency 1.0 enables you to select a color within a gif to make transparent: reverting to the gray background example, you would make the gray colors in your graphic transparent. The graphic appears to float on any page, not just gray pages.

Summary

The remainder of this book is a primer on exercising basic usability, basic design practice, and some on-the-fly creativity. Different template models are reviewed that were created with specific web site content in mind—from text-rich content to highly interactive sites. Each chapter will discuss usability considerations for a particular type of content, what a web site backend is and how it can be set up to make the tasks of creating, accessing, and storing files much easier. Each template model within the chapter will point out elements that make the template successful and offer HTML writing tips to duplicate the effect; for full code and docsourcing, you can review the CD-ROM that accompanies this book.

And now, on to the templates, and to the tools that will make managing a mountain seem more like managing a molehill.

CHAPTER 3

Text-Heavy Materials

What this chapter covers:

❖ What Content Fits into the Text-Intensive Category
❖ Template Considerations for Text-Intensive Projects
❖ Templates for:

- ◆ Annual Reports
- ◆ Business Plans and Prospecti
- ◆ Peer-Reviewed Published Papers and Studies
- ◆ Magazine Articles
- ◆ Reference Resources

Your boss has just dropped a hundred-page annual report on your desk and asked, very nicely, that you have it put on the web by the time the board of directors meets. The meeting is six days away. You:

1. Resist the urge to break into maniacal laughter, and mentally cancel your plans for the next five nights.
2. Begin fine-tuning your resume, and mentally cancel your plans for the next five nights.
3. Quickly review the report's content, map the content to a rough directory structure, and begin working on a template that will enable you to drop 100 pages of text with relatively few errors.

The answer, of course, is number three, and not just because this book advocates using templates. Dealing with large amounts of text may seem daunting no matter what, but most content can be broken down into smaller chunks of text, and from there it's only a matter of developing a workable file tree, using this structure to design a template that reflects the content sorting, and completing the project piece-by-piece.

What Content Fits into the Text-Intensive Category?

You can usually surmise if a proposed web site is going to be text intensive by evaluating the following factors:

❖ Volume of the original material
❖ Purpose of the original material
❖ Potential accumulation of the material
❖ Inherent text-intensive nature of the material

The most obvious consideration for a text-intensive project is the volume of the material—60 pages of text qualifies as text-intensive. Not all the material has to be present at the start of the project, but rather, consider the possibility of the volume growing.

Another consideration is the purpose of the material. Archival sites, online publications, and reference directories all contain large amounts of information, much of it in text format. If the site is going to be providing a lot of information—and that information is all part of a large body of work—it falls into the category of a text-intensive project.

A third consideration is accumulation of material. If the validity of the contents depends on all the material being available at once, or new material being added to existing material, then the project can be considered information-intensive—and very likely text intensive. A body of work that accumulates over time, or acts as an archival resource, definitely falls into the text-intensive category.

All three considerations assume that the contents of the web site will expand over time; however, projects like annual reports, doctoral theses, or other one-time postings may contain a lot of material. These types of elements also fall into the text-intensive category.

For examples of text-intensive sites already on the web, visit the following:

- ❖ **The Gutenberg Project** (`http://www.promo.net/pg/`): this online archive had the complete text of over 900 books online as of May 4, 1997.
- ❖ **IUPAC Nomenclature of Organic Chemistry** (`http://www.acdlabs.com/iupac/nomenclature/`): this is a wonderful, branching text reference with a clear hierarchy of information.
- ❖ **The Utne Web** (`http://www.utne.com`): proof that text-intensive does not equal boredom.

Template Considerations for Text-Intensive Projects

The sheer volume of content in a text-intensive web site can be daunting, but that's where careful template design comes in to play. To make sure the initial planning and template coding are an efficient tool and not a waste of time, this chapter analyzes how a template can work with the features of a text-heavy site, and how this will translate into web page design and overall site construction.

The recommended steps for building a web site based on a text-intensive body of work are as follows:

1. Quickly review the content.
2. Begin to map the file structure behind the site.
3. Determine how to navigate that file structure.
4. Set the look and feel of the content.
5. Set aside a sufficient amount of time for content formatting.

Quickly Review the Content

Quickly reviewing the content doesn't mean that you should painstakingly read it—go through chapters or sections and list them. Note how many different types of information are contained in the body of work, such as charts, text chapters, illustrative diagrams, indices, definitions, and so on. The point is to get a handle on how many different types of information you'll need to consider in building the site, and to understand how they relate to each other.

Begin to Map the File Structure Behind the Site

After you've identified any natural organizational structures in the document, and cataloged how many types of information you'll have to present, begin to map the file structure behind the site. Take advantage of the categories you've identified, and use them as preliminary dividing lines in the content. If, for example, you're posting a doctoral thesis online, you could break up the content into three areas: chapters, references, and diagrams. When you begin to build your back end file structure, you may decide to give each chapter a separate directory, so that your back end looks like figure 3.1.

Figure 3.1

Mapping the site directory structure.

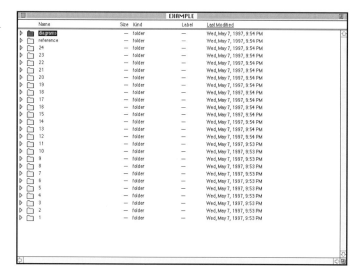

After you've set up this structure, you can sort and divide the content—each has a content-specific, type-specific place to live. Separating the content is advisable for a few reasons:

❖ It enables you to divide the work into manageable chunks.

❖ You can reference the different types of information when you begin to design your template.

❖ It forces you to commit to a structure and move ahead to the next step of planning your web site.

Determine How to Navigate the File Structure

The next step is, of course, to determine how to navigate the file structure. Fortunately, because you physically mapped the file structure, the technical considerations are already done. What you should decide now is how to present the division of information in a way that your readers understand how each section is connected to the other sections. Remember, this project is one big chunk of cohesive content—your job is to make the manageable chunks blend together in an intuitive navigation device.

A few ways to do this are content-related. Set up your navigational device to reflect a hierarchy of information, if that's appropriate. You can set up a toolbar that shows the user the different types of content.

> **Always be sure that your navigational tool permits the user to know where he is within the site, and that it shows the reader how the content he is reading relates to the whole site.**

Returning to our doctoral thesis example, the student in question might set their navigation bar to reflect a few different levels of content. The introductory bar might run down the left-hand margin of the page and look like figure 3.2.

Figure 3.2

Using a textual navigation bar to organize content and navigate the web site.

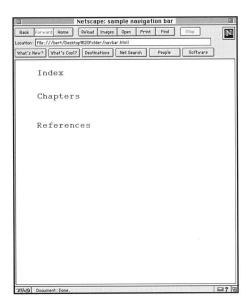

As a reader clicks on Chapters, the bar might change (see fig. 3.3).

Figure 3.3

Using a navigation bar to present information hierarchically.

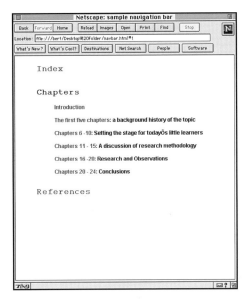

In the case of the first navigation bar, "Chapters" was linked to `<introduction.html>`, the introductory page for the chapters. After the reader connects to that page, the reader can then click on "The first five chapters" to display a navigation bar with even more specific information.

The navigation bar becomes more complex as the reader drills down into the site, but with careful design, it can still maintain the look and feel that identifies it as an information tool, and contains the information well. Note that the hierarchy of information is successfully communicated at every level. Indenting worked in this case, but you do the same thing with font size, font face, or color. Use layout elements to visually reinforce how the information is organized.

Set the Look and Feel of the Content

The next part of building your template is to set the look and feel of the content. If you're dealing with clearly hierarchical information, you can take advantage of that by setting up visual cues that parallel that hierarchy: different font sizes to start different sections, differing degrees of indentation, or material that is hyperlinked off the main category but not linked to anything else in the site (a back-and-forth link). You will be spending a lot of time formatting your content, so decide early how to do so.

Set Aside a Sufficient Amount of Time for Content Formatting

Estimate and set aside a sufficient amount of time for content formatting: the volume of material is high, and you will have to make it fit within your established file structure and web page interface. Even if a lot of your early template-to-web site work is simple cut-and-paste, you'll still have to go back later and check for the following:

❖ Does every chunk of content live in a place on the site that makes sense?

❖ Is that placement reflected in how the content is formatted?

❖ Are styles consistent across every section of content? Even if those sections are internally consistent, are they consistent across the site?

❖ Does the visual transition from one section to another keep the reader oriented within the site? Are there any visual features that are not consistent from section to section?

❖ Have you proofread the content to make sure you didn't leave out any sections by mistake?

❖ Do all the links work?

In other words, a good template will save you setup time, but don't forget to budget time for proofreading.

But the good news is you won't have to spend a lot of time updating the content. Even if the site is built for archival purposes, or you plan on adding new material weekly, the hardest part is already over—setting up a file structure, determining a framework for the content, and building an interface that guides your user through a large amount of content.

A second piece of good news is that you won't have to spend a lot of time incorporating user interactivity into your site. The reason for the site is analogous to publishing—to get information out to the public. If you want user feedback, e-mail links are painless, quick, and easy to incorporate into a site. It's not as if I'm discounting the user-engaging strengths of the web: you will be spending your time working on structuring the site so that your users can have a full navigational/editorial experience. The type of user participation that you're aiming for here can be thought of as the web equivalent of a self-guided museum tour. You spend your time creating cool exhibits and a museum map; your user decides what cool exhibit to visit, and uses your map to get there.

The remainder of the chapter has specific template examples of text-intensive web sites that consist of the following:

❖ **Annual Reports:** Often found on business-oriented or organizational web sites, annual reports are a way to sum up a year's worth of organizational activity and provide lasting background material on the organization.

❖ **Business Plans and Prospecti:** These documents contain financial data listing an organization's assets, liabilities, income, expenditures, and budgetary projections. They are a source of financial data and a way to see potential investors of a company.

❖ **Peer-Reviewed/Published Papers and Studies:** Tricky to format because they often have footnotes, annotations, and other easy-to-miss chunks of data that are integral to the reading experience. These are usually posted on academic or technology-industry sites (think of White Papers).

❖ **Magazine Articles:** These are usually part of a larger body of work, such as a publication site.

❖ **Reference Resources:** These can be anything from an index of other web resources to a phonebook like file of names, people, places, and things. The W3 standards come to mind as a reference site.

> **NOTE**
> For full-color representations of the templates, access the CD-ROM that accompanies this book.

Figure 3_a_01

This traditional layout works well because the layout is hemmed in by a company masthead and a navigation bar, and is set narrowly enough to work on a small screen. The margin is set by careful <TABLE CELLSPACING>, a trick that works best when the table isn't used to align a heavy graphic layout.

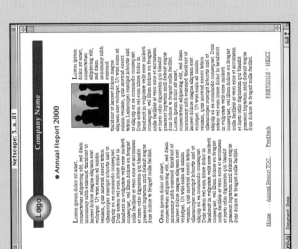

Figure 3_a_02

This is a slightly more feature-heavy variation of a basic layout. Notice how the font denotes different information tools: sans serif for topical headlines, bold serif echoing the content and emphasizing key content chunks. Remember: the font attributes are your friends–use them to establish and reinforce a consistent information hierarchy.

Figure 3_a_03

A third variation on the basic layout; notice that you can use the BORDER tag to set individual table cells. This will work best in browsers that support HTML 3.0.

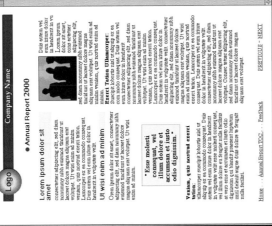

Figure 3_a_04

More fun with individual table tags. This template focuses on the attributes of individual table cells: subheads are set off with <TD BGCOLOR> tags, as is the pull quote.The pull quote is set apart with a <TD BORDER = 1> tag. Note the font attributes and how they correspond to different levels in the information hierarchy—sans serif and burgundy for subheads, bold and serif to emphasize elements within the content.

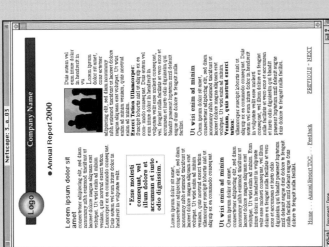

Figure 3_b_01

This is a good layout for documents with multiple sections. Notice the index on the left does not intrude on the content, but combines nicely with the vertical margin to define the body of the site. The low-bandwidth vertical margin is one table cell set to multiple columns and filled in with a different background color.

Figure 3_b_02

The index page is neatly organized by differing font attributes. The key to doing this successfully is to maintain a clear and consistent link between the visual code and the corresponding content.

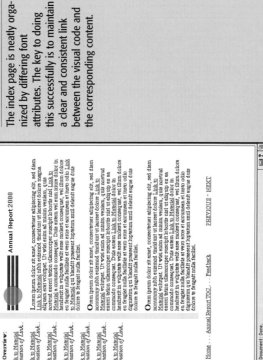

Figure 3_b_03

This is a good basic layout for documents that are conspicuously structured for hypertext. The links are clearly delineated with the different font size and face, yet not too obtrusive.

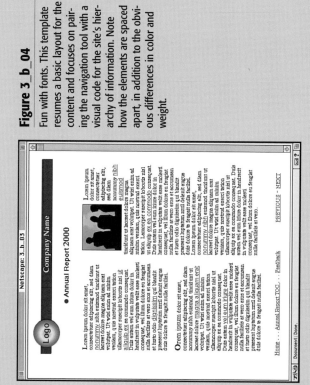

Figure 3_b_04

Fun with fonts. This template resumes a basic layout for the content and focuses on pairing the navigation tool with a visual code for the site's hierarchy of information. Note how the elements are spaced apart, in addition to the obvious differences in color and weight.

Indexed and Crosslinked Documents

Figure 3_b_05

This is a good layout for people targeting low-resolution audiences and small screens. The compact layout relies on the relation of three main elements: the navigation bar, the indented blockquote, and the body copy—note how they all maintain a strong vertical line.

Netscape: 3_b_05

Annual Report 2000

Index:

Link to Material
ipsum dolor sit amet, consectetur adipiscing elit
Link to Material
ipsum dolor sit amet,
consectetur adipiscing elit
Link to Material
ipsum dolor sit amet,
consectetur adipiscing elit
Link to Material
ipsum dolor sit amet,
consectetur adipiscing elit
Link to Material
ipsum dolor sit amet,
consectetur adipiscing elit

Lorem ipsum dolor sit amet, consectetuer adipiscing elit, sed diam aliquam erat volutpat. Ut wisi enim ad minim veniam, quis nostrud exerci tation ullamcorper suscipit lobortis nisl Link to Material a commodo consequat. Duis autem vel eum iriure dolor in hendrerit in vulputate velit esse molesti consequat, vel illum dolore eu feugiat nulla facilisis at vero eros et accumsan et iusto odio Link to Material qui blandit praesent luptatum zzril delenit augue duis dolore te feugait nulla facilisi.

Orem ipsum dolor sit amet, consectetuer adipiscing elit, sed diam nonummy nibh euismod tincidunt ut laoreet dolore Link to Material to Material volutpat. Ut wisi enim ad minim veniam, qui nostrud exerci tation ullamcorper suscipit lobortis nisl ut aliquip ex ea commodo consequat. Duis autem Link to Material dolor in hendrerit in vulputate velit esse molesti consequat, vel illum dolore eu feugiat nulla facilisis at vero eros et accumsan et iusto odio dignissim qui blandit praesent luptatum zzril delenit augue duis dolore te feugait nulla facilisi.

Orem ipsum dolor sit amet, consectetuer adipiscing elit, sed diam nonummy nibh euismod tincidunt ut laoreet dolore Link to Material volutpat. Ut wisi enim ad minim veniam, quis nostrud exerci tation ullamcorper suscipit lobortis nisl ut aliquip ex ea commodo consequat. Duis autem Link to Material illum dolore eu feugiat nulla facilisis at vero eros et accumsan et iusto odio dignissim qui blandit praesent luptatum zzril delenit augue duis dolore te feugait nulla facilisi.

Home · · Annual Report TOC · · Feedback   PREVIOUS · NEXT

Figure 3_b_06

Focus on font sizes as a direct indicator of hierarchy of information: the captions take a smaller role than main content, and the content is differentiated by raised capitals. This font size variation, paired with a simple table layout, works well across any browser that supports HTML 2.0 or better.

Netscape: 3_b_06

Annual Report 2000

Link to Material
Explanation of Link...
Link to Material
Explanation of Link...
Link to Material
Explanation of Link...
Link to Material
Explanation of Link...
Link to Material
Explanation of Link...

Lorem ipsum dolor sit amet, consectetuer adipiscing elit, sed diam Link to Material nibh euismod tincidunt ut laoreet dolore magna aliquam erat volutpat. Ut wisi enim ad minim veniam, quis nostrud exerci tation ullamcorper suscipit lobortis nisl Link to Material a commodo consequat. Duis autem vel eum iriure dolor in hendrerit in vulputate velit esse molesti consequat, vel illum dolore eu feugiat nulla facilisis at vero eros et accumsan et iusto odio Link to Material qui blandit praesent luptatum zzril delenit augue duis dolore te feugait nulla facilisi.

Orem ipsum dolor sit amet, consectetuer adipiscing elit, sed diam nonummy nibh euismod tincidunt ut laoreet dolore Link to Material volutpat. Ut wisi enim ad minim veniam, quis nostrud exerci tation ullamcorper suscipit lobortis nisl ut aliquip ex ea commodo consequat. Duis autem Link to Material dolor in hendrerit in vulputate velit esse molesti consequat, vel illum dolore eu feugiat nulla facilisis at vero eros et accumsan et iusto odio dignissim qui blandit praesent luptatum zzril delenit augue duis dolore te feugait nulla facilisi.

Orem ipsum dolor sit amet, consectetuer adipiscing elit, sed diam nonummy nibh euismod tincidunt ut laoreet dolore Link to Material volutpat. Ut wisi enim ad minim veniam, quis nostrud exerci tation ullamcorper suscipit lobortis nisl ut aliquip ex ea commodo consequat. Duis autem Link to Material dolor in hendrerit in vulputate velit esse molesti consequat, vel illum dolore eu feugiat nulla facilisis at vero eros et accumsan et iusto odio dignissim qui blandit praesent luptatum zzril delenit augue duis dolore te feugait nulla facilisi.

Framed, Indexed, and Crosslinked Documents

Figure 3_c_01

This frames layout is deceptively simple for the reader—a good thing in this case. The navigation bar at the left is one file calling content to load into the right. The link at the bottom returns the user to the home frame via <TARGET = "mainframe">. The seamless look was accomplished by adding an attribute to the frameset tag: <FRAMESET BORDER = 0>.

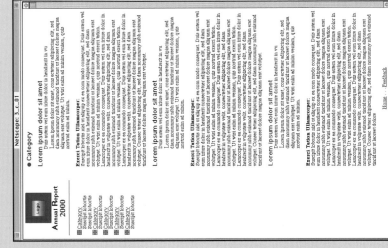

Figure 3_c_02

A slightly more graphic-intensive layout. An image map works best if you have a clear file tree and don't need to worry about updating the map frequently. The body content establishes and maintains a clear visual hierarchy of information via the font face, size, and color. It works well because the navigation bar picks it up and graphically reinforces it too.

ANNUAL REPORTS

Framed, Indexed, and Crosslinked Documents

Figure 3_c_03

A horizontal frames layout is good for positioning two different and significant elements. In this case, the body copy is the primary focus, but the generously sized navigation bar notifies the reader that the document is one part of a much larger web site.

Figure 3_c_04

Notice the difference between placing the frame at the bottom of the page instead of at the top. In the last frame, the navigation bar was at the bottom, lending the content page primary status—in this case, the navigation bar is obviously the focus of the site—it's a constant from page to page—and the content is a part of the larger site structure.

Figure 3_c_05

Three seamless frames are at work here—the top left-hand frame has the logo for the company (it can be any element that is meant to be constant from layout to layout), the lower-left hand frame is a navigational device, and the content loads in the frame on the right side of the page. The seamless frames (accomplished with <FRAMESET BORDER = 0>) duplicate a page layout, but the navigation bar arrangement enables you to exploit hypertext as a means of presenting large amounts of content.

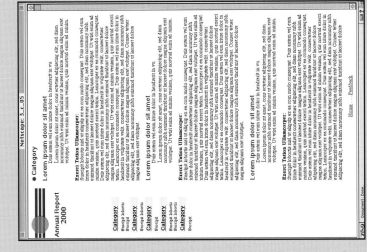

Figure 3_c_06

The frames here are delineated with a <BORDER = 1 BORDERCOLOR = ""> tag—which may not work across browsers that do not support HTML 3.0. Still, the layout provides a great visual way to present two different navigation bars. The top navigation bar deals with the site as a whole, and the bottom presents the links within the content document to the right. The way to distinguish these bars from each other is to change the background color of the smaller-scale one to make it less prominent. The content-specific navigation bar is tied to the content via a color scheme that is reflected in both the navigation bar and the content page.

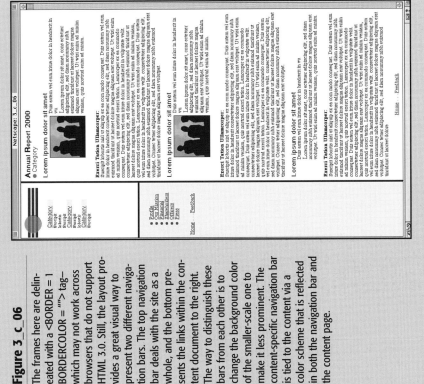

Text-Intensive Straight Documents

Figure 3_d_01

A traditional layout. Note how project-wide contents—head-line, company name, logo, and navigation bar—are clustered together as the chief visual identifier. This enables you to swap in any type of formatted content below the distinctive visual feature.

Other touches are the parallel color schemes and font faces used for headlines and sub-heads, and a company logo color picked up as the color for all the page hyperlinks.

Figure 3_d_02

Mixing and matching fonts helps create a clear distinction between site-wide visual traits and content-specific ones. Notice that links are bold to help them stand out more. This is a good layout for text-intensive content. The sans serif font looks roomier, but the courier font keeps the page from looking like a Tomorrowland pamphlet.

Figure 3_d_03

The navigation bar was created in a slightly lighter color than the content—this helps separate it visually. Note that only the table cells were highlighted—this way, the navigation bar still appears to be an organic part of the site. To further reinforce the layout, the vertical eyeline that the navigation bar bumps against also pulls together the company masthead and the content.

Figure 3_d_04

This layout works for a few reasons. The palette is kept simple, with extra-content features in blue and links in red. Second, there's a strong vertical line that keeps all the elements pulled along the same eyepath. Third, a clear hierarchy of information is established via the different font sizes and font faces—content in times and page elements in courier.

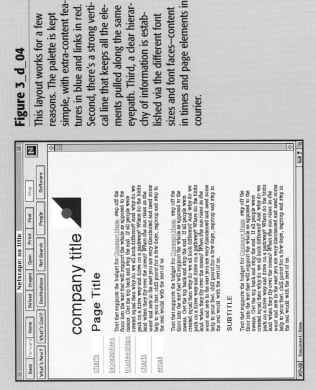

BUSINESS PLANS AND PROSPECTI

50/50 Mixed Text and Charts

Figure 3_e_01

A solid and consistent color scheme, strong left margins, and clearly defined chunks of information all contribute to the report's easy readability. This layout also degrades well across different browsers—the table, font color, and font sizes will all show up in 1995-era browsers.

Figure 3_e_02

Strong color blocks enable the layout to present two distinct and complete chunks of content on one screen without relying on frames. The layout also works because the uniform layout of elements denotes some sort of relationship between the two items while establishing that they can also stand on their own. Although this is one way to get around loading three files, note that it only works on browsers that support HTML 3.0, or higher.

Figure 3_e_03

The graphic and sidebar stacked together help to establish the contextual relevance of each item to the whole layout and they enable the main body text to stand out on the page. The whole layout works because the strong margins and generous eyespace pull the elements into balance with one another, rather than clumping together on the page.

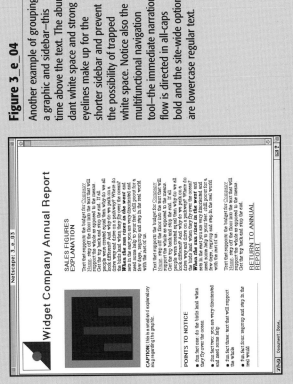

Figure 3_e_04

Another example of grouping a graphic and sidebar—this time above the text. The abundant white space and strong eyelines make up for the shorter sidebar and prevent the possibility of trapped white space. Notice also the multifunctional navigation tool—the immediate narration flow is directed in all-caps bold and the site-wide options are lowercase regular text.

50/50 Mixed Text and Charts

Figure 3_e_05

An example of horizontal use of color to visually denote different elements on the page. The horizontal approach works better than the vertical approach when the data is better presented across a page (like a graphic) or if the items are brief enough where several can be stacked without the reader feeling as though the page is squishing items. Remember to provide textual and spatial cues separating the different chunks of information, so that users who are viewing your site through older browsers can still understand how you organized the information.

Figure 3_e_06

A nice use of color to punch up an otherwise standard report layout. Note that the color accents the visual/graphic section of the layout—be sure to use a color that doesn't distract, overwhelm, or clash with the visuals—or you lose the whole point of adding color in the first place. Be sure also to maintain spatial cues like strong margins, so that lower-end users can still see why you laid out the information as you did.

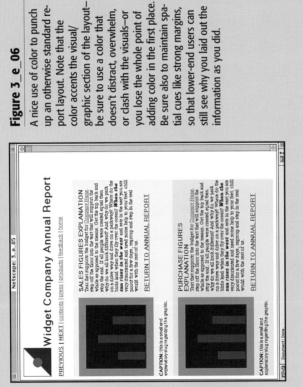

Figure 3_f_01

The page contains two key categories of information—data and data interpretation. The two are sharply distinguished in this example by the use of different font attributes. All data is bold blue sans serif and all data interpretation is in a standard times font. The layout also chunks together data and results, thus enabling a natural flow of information.

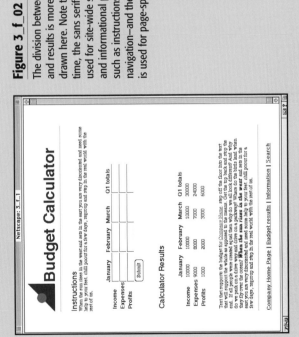

Figure 3_f_02

The division between options and results is more sharply drawn here. Note that this time, the sans serif font is used for site-wide structure and informational purposes—such as instructions and site navigation—and the serif font is used for page-specific data.

Figure 3_f_03

The primary focus of this layout is the proverbial picture that's worth a thousand words—or one web site. Why does this work? Users have a clear idea of cause-and-effect with selecting a graph variable and reading the results. The strong horizontal lines that box the data explanation away from the rest of the site also serve to highlight its status as the logical result of a user's selection.

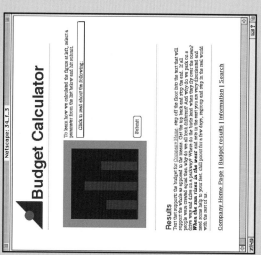

Figure 3_f_04

Another picture worth a thousand words. The different selection means (radio buttons) allow the top graph and user option to be chunked together tightly. This also allows for more space between the selection and the results. Notice that the font scheme is still strictly divided along functional lines—sans serif for site-wide information and options, and serif fonts for page-specific data.

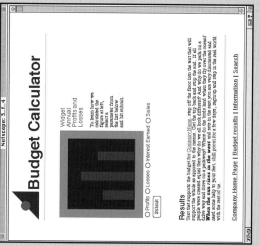

Figure 3_f_05

Multiple options for the user are displayed with minimum confusion at the top of the page. The pull-down menu ensures that all the options for each criteria are available without overwhelming the reader.

Budget Calculator

Widget Annual Profits and Losses
To determine the financial security you have, select a parameter from the list below and hit submit.

January   [Click to read about the following:]
February [Click to read about the following:]
March   [Click to read about the following:]
Q1 totals [Click to read about the following:]
          [Submit]

Results
Text that supports the budget for Company Name, step off the floor into the text that will support the whole as supposed to the menus. Get the toy back and stop the end. If all people were created equal then why do we all look different? And why do we pack on a drive way and drive on a parkway? Where do the birds land when they fly over the ocean? *When the sun rises in the west* and sets in the east you are very disoriented and need some help to your feet. chill pount for a few days, regroup and step in the real world with the rest of us.

Company Home Page | Budget results | Information | Search

Figure 3_f_06

This template represents a slightly higher degree of user interactivity. The user can now enter criteria that she wants to analyze, and the results are spatially and typographically distinct from the variables.

Budget Calculator

1. enter the state you live in
   [CA]
2. enter your zip code
   [   ]
3. enter your email address
   [   ]
   [Submit]

Text that supports the budget for Company Name, step off the floor into the text that will support the whole as supposed to the menus. Get the toy back and stop the end. If all people were created equal then why do we all look different? And why do we pack on a drive way and drive on a parkway? Where do the birds land when they fly over the ocean? *When the sun rises in the west* and sets in the east you are very disoriented and need some help to your feet. chill pount for a few days, regroup and step in the real world with the rest of us.

Company Home Page | Budget results | Information | Search

BUSINESS PLANS AND PROSPECTI

Framed and Crosslinked Documents

Figure 3_g_01

Frames enable a clear visual separation between the user-driven part of the site and the information presented as a result of the user's choices. The total layout is still pulled together because of a strong and consistent left margin and consistent use of font attributes to establish the roles of different chunks of information on the site.

Figure 3_g_02

The consistent color scheme ties together the results frame and the user-choice frame so that the documents don't look unrelated. The data represented in each are different though—so the different font sizes and faces establish that.

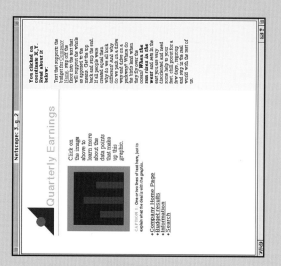

Figure 3_g_03

The consistent color scheme and font hierarchy helps to establish visual consistency between the two pages. Note that the results load into the left in a smaller font, thus adding to—not distracting from—the main picture on the page.

Figure 3_g_04

Navigation and interactivity for the power user—the full array of navigation options stay constant on the left, and the frame at the bottom changes depending on the selection that the user makes in the main frame. This layout succeeds with careful frame targeting (be sure to note what your frame names are!) and consistent color schemes in all three windows.

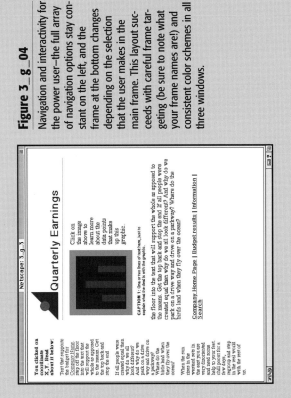

Figure 3_g_05

This is another take on the power-user layout. The advantage to having the navigation options at the top of the page is that any selections load into the main frame immediately below it–a solid visual flow of information from user selection to resulting content. If you're going to use multiple frames, remember to leave enough room around each section so that it is allowed to serve a distinct visual role within a larger page, not just get lost in a blur of content.

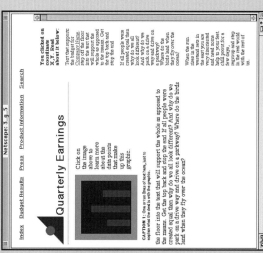

Figure 3_g_06

The content window is distinguished from the data explanation and site navigation windows via background colors–provided you stay within the same palette, mixing background color can provide strong visual impact and can convey different information functions on a framed site.

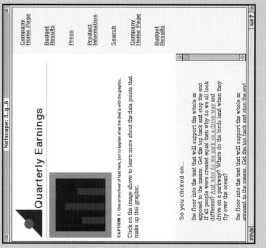

Figure 3_g_07

This is another take on varying background colors, this time with a reversed layout. Notice how this seems to pull the content window into a bigger picture, as opposed to setting it apart. Exploit the browser's left-down orientation if you want to closely pack related frames together in a layout.

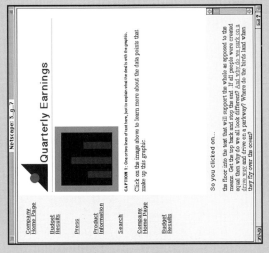

Figure 3_g_08

A basic two-frame layout, punched up with a mixing and matching of different font faces. Note that the fonts still convey very function-specific information. Site information is visually distinguishable from page information.

Figure 3_h_01

The dual columns reflect a traditional paper structure nicely, and ensure that the reader does has some visual "breathing space." Note also how the paper navigation tools are visually distinct from the site navigation tools, thus setting up both a means of organizing the content and a means for navigating the site.

Figure 3_h_02

The navigation is moved to the top of the page, enabling users to see where the content fits in relation to the site. The clear paper navigation remains at the bottom of the page—a context-sensitive design decision.

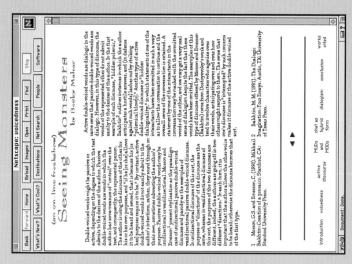

Figure 3_h_03

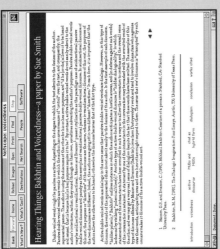

This layout works well because of the mix in fonts—each differently formatted section has an obvious and discrete purpose—and in the use of space to prevent the layout from getting blocky or cluttered. Aligning the internal navigation structure to the right is a good design move that helps the graphics stand out, and alleviates the strong horizontal lines.

Figure 3_h_04

A clear relationship between color and content is illustrated in this template. Content-related information is set to the right, which follows a tendency to read left-to-right, and site-wide information is blocked off to the left. Note also that information useful on a site-wide basis, such as where one may be, is set apart from the content chunks via font faces.

Figure 3_h_05

The footnotes were aligned to the top to prevent the appearance of any trapped white space. The color scheme is what prevents the footnotes from getting equal visual billing—the dark content block and title bars draw the eye more readily. An advantage to having the footnotes aligned at the top is that a subtle visual connection is made between the auxiliary content and the main content that it is bumping against.

Figure 3_h_06

The small, clean fonts and careful spacing prevent this template from looking like one of those scary pamphlets that you get with over-the-counter medicine. This good, basic layout degrades well across browsers.

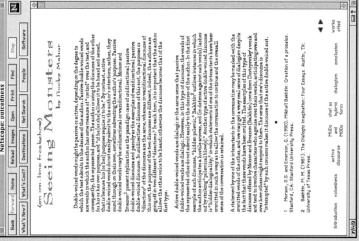

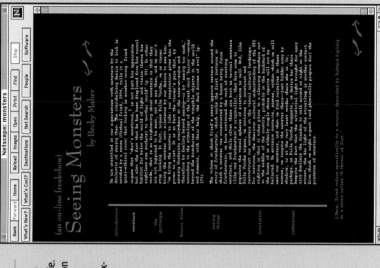

3_i_01

Color makes this layout. The navigation is set in a vibrant contrasting palette, enabling the user to easily find it, and also allowing the possibility of color-coding sections for subtle visual reinforcement. Other good layout features are a strong vertical eyeline, and a footnote spanning both navigation and content, which enables the items to be tied together visually.

Figure 3_i_02

This is a more saturated example. The eyeline is further reinforced with the green rule. In this layout, any information that is not directly related to the text is green. This can be an effective visual way of boxing in the main content.

Footnoted, Crosslinked, and Referenced Documents

Figure 3_i_03

An effective use of space and color to frame content is illustrated in this example. The presentation of content in the white window ensures its readability. The navigation device contrasts both in font (thus creating a subtle spatial difference) and color. Note that the footnote font is still the same as the content font, subtly reinforcing the tie between the two.

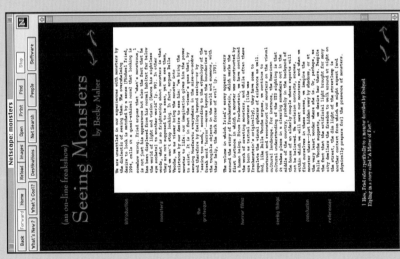

Figure 3_i_04

Another take on the contrasting-color content box. In this case, the spaces are a little tighter and more strictly defined. The advantage to this is that it fits well across a great variety of screens. There's also a subtle difference in the color scheme. Note that only the you-are-here link is colored, in contrast to the entire navigation bar being colored.

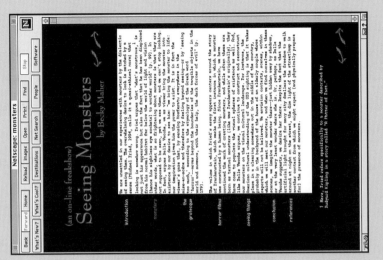

Figure 3_i_05

A more horizontal layout. In this example, color is used to distinguish between different content types. Here, the main content is featured in white. Footnotes—auxiliary information that is directly related to main content—are also featured in white. The navigation bars break the white content correlation and appear in color. Note two things about the navigation bar: the color is coded so that you know where you are, and, because the page can be long, the navigation bar is repeated at the top and bottom of the page.

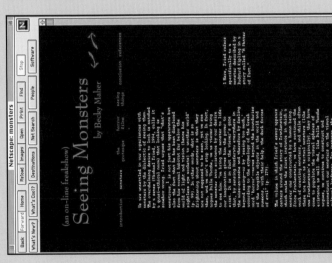

Figure 3_i_06

Even more use of color in a horizontal context—the text is pulled out of the layout by framing it in a 180-degree switch on the site color scheme. This works well because no other distracting visual elements are on the site. The rest of the layout is very plain, and there is no mix-and-match of fonts. Note that the footnote still stays tied in because it appears in the same color scheme (albeit reversed) as the main text.

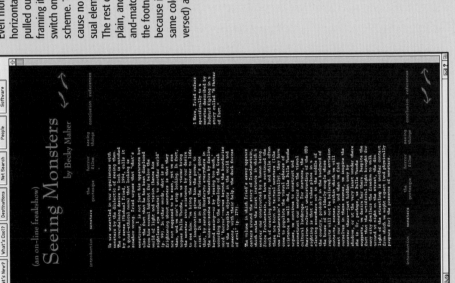

Figure 3_i_07

In this example, the color layout is given some help by mixing and matching fonts. Note the use of fonts to establish information hierarchy probably wouldn't work as well if dramatic color blocking was the main use for contrasting colors. The different fonts help to separate content-specific information from site-wide information.

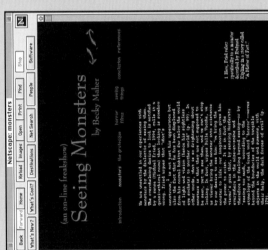

Figure 3_i_08

Footnotes are tucked neatly into text without interrupting narrative flow. The font and font color remained the same, providing stylistic consistency through the whole content section. This consistency was further reinforced by keeping the footnote width the same as the content width. The only contrast—setting off the footnote with color—works because the color ties into the navigational devices and sends the visual signal that this information is auxiliary to the content.

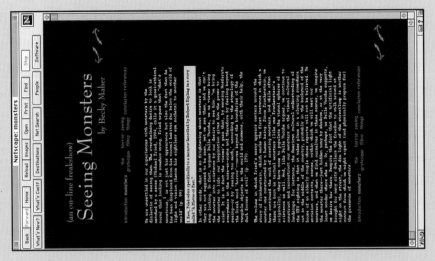

Figure 3_i_09

The recursive navigation bars are a great way to refresh the reader on what the narrative flow is, and what the user's navigation options are. The navigation bars are also set off in contrasting colors, which cues the user to their different functions. Note that the simplicity of the layout is what makes this design so successful—if it were graphically rich, it would be too dense and confusing to navigate.

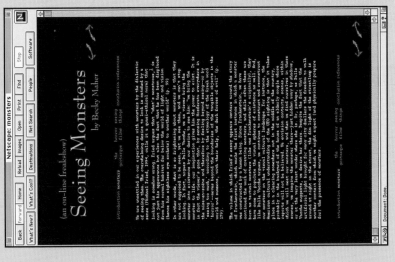

Figure 3_j_01

The navigation functions are in gray and the page-specific content is in white. The color coding reinforces the different functions each frame plays in this layout. The advantage to using so many frames is that it enables the reader to have greater control over the flow of information (provided you targeted your windows correctly) and allows you to change content without having to alter every navigational trait on the site.

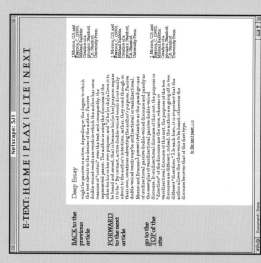

Figure 3_j_02

The navigational aspect of the layout has different coloring and a different font hierarchy. This is useful in establishing a site-wide look and feel through several lengththy informational and content paths. Note that the content has its own hierarchy of information set up by the different font sizes, and that the two different chunks of information are tied together by color scheme and font face.

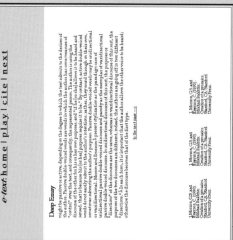

Figure 3_j_03

The content carves a larger space in the monitor with this four-frame iteration. A more horizontal layout might be more effective if you're presenting content that relies on a continuous visual line to be understood (such as graphs or spreadsheets), or if the ancillary content (footnotes or sidebars) can be presented well in small portions.

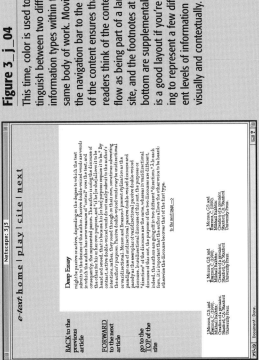

Figure 3_j_04

This time, color is used to distinguish between two different information types within the same body of work. Moving the navigation bar to the top of the content ensures that readers think of the content flow as being part of a larger site, and the footnotes at the bottom are supplemental. This is a good layout if you're trying to represent a few different levels of information both visually and contextually.

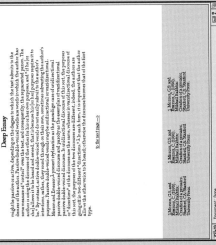

Figure 3_j_05

A sharp visual contrast between the bold navigation bar and the airy content layout. This is a good layout for establishing and maintaining the idea that the content is a subdirectory of a larger site tree, and that the other branches of the tree are also readily accessible. Note that the two different parts of the page still share a color scheme and font face, tying them together subtly.

Figure 3_j_06

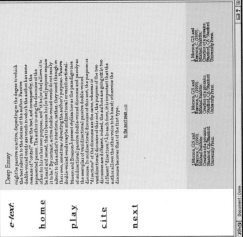

Slightly different colors help denote different informational functions within one document. Note how the two most closely related colors correspond with the most closely related information. Elements tying all three pages together are the total color scheme and the clear establishment and maintenance of one font hierarchy across three different pages.

Figure 3_j_07

This time, the color is used to mark information that can re-move the reader from the file tree. The file tree itself is de-noted and reinforced in the white layout—the levels of the tree are clearly shown via different font sizes.

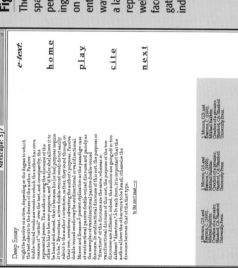

Figure 3_j_08

The sharp horizontal layout, spaces, and contrasting colors perform the function of show-ing that the content can stand on its own away from the par-ent web site. This is a good way to tie in microsites within a larger site, such as special reports or event-generated web sites. Note that the font face and size still tie the navi-gation bar into the quasi-independent site.

MAGAZINE ARTICLES

Straight Text

Figure 3_k_01

The related text is shown as part of the layout, yet remains functionally separate by means of a different font and a much smaller space on the page. The reverse color scheme helps point out that the content is tied into the main page, and the font sizes establish the contents place in the site's overall hierarchy of information.

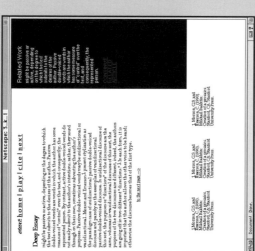

Figure 3_k_02

A non-frames way to incorporate different and related text into a complete page is to use table cell colors to set the content apart. To back-engineer this for browsers that don't support HTML 3.0, make the font face and color distinct from the main body fonts (use <TT>, for example) and consider using horizontal rules to set the boundaries on the sidebar.

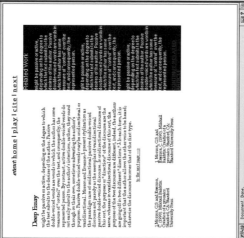

Figure 3_|_01

The sans serif font is used to connote content categories, and the varying indents correspond to the content the template is trying to emphasize. Because the margins are the primary visual interest here, there is only one extra color, used for hyperlinks and heading.

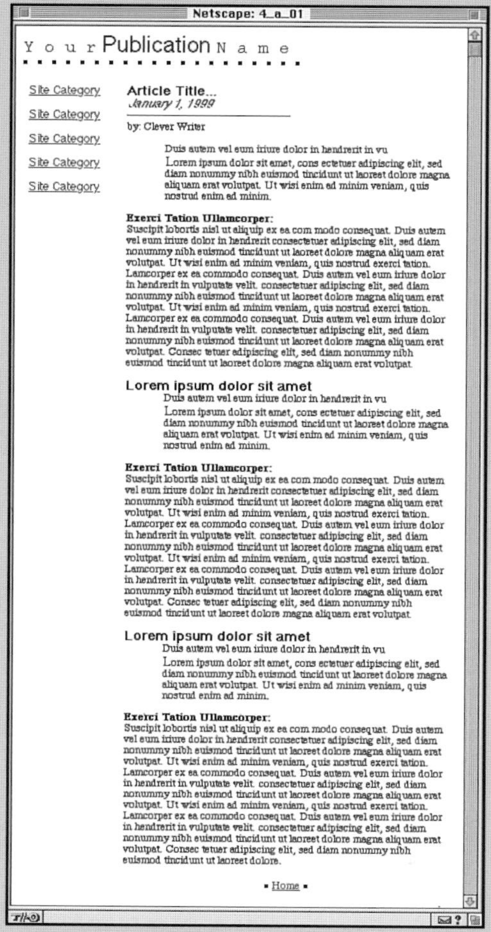

Figure 3_|_02

A conservative layout, livened with a pull quote. Notice again that sans serif font is used to indicate information relevant to the site as a whole—navigation options and content titles—but the pull quote is in the same font as the content. This is a subtle visual way of tying the visually distinct item to the parent content.

Figure 3_l_03

Fun with fonts! Notice that the pull quote is now in sans serif font like the rest of the site-specific elements, instead of being in the same font as the page-specific content. This ensures a nice visual continuity, even if the pull quote and content are separated. Either tactic (this one or the preceding one) will work within the site as whole—you just have to decide whether or not you place greater priority on site-wide visual continuity or one content continuity. (There is no correct answer.)

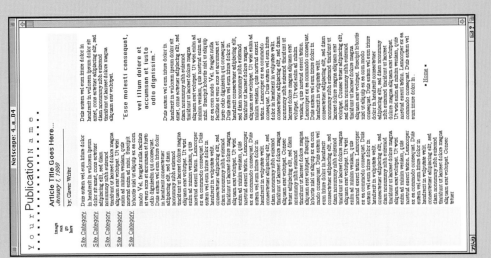

Figure 3_l_04

Notice how the colored table cells serve two functions. They set the site-wide information elements (navigation bar, page title) aside from the content, and they box in the content neatly, allowing a clear, visually distinct layout.

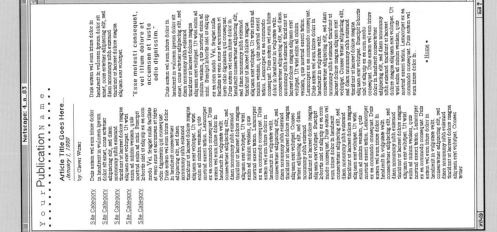

Figure 3_m_01

A new element is introduced to the layout in this design—a list of links related to the content. Notice how the list is set apart from the content visually, but the font is consistent with the body copy. These two visual cues may seem contradictory but they do the job of establishing the visual list as a separate information section while providing context for the stuff in the list. This was all done via a table—one for the link list embedded within one for the page layout.

Figure 3_m_02

Another use of tables to align elements, the one-row, multi-celled table lines up links neatly, and the code can be moved, modified, or deleted quickly. Looking more closely at the table you'll notice how color and font are used to establish a visual hierarchy of information. This is picked up and reinforced through the rest of the site: sans serif font for information items that are consistently included through the site, and serif for the body text.

Figure 3_m_03

A basic layout accomplished via tables. The related links list is set apart using only table cell colors.

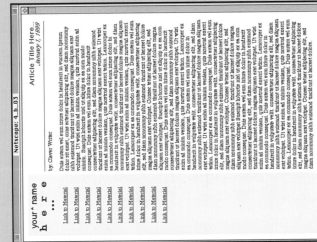

Figure 3_m_04

This is a good way to break up a lot of text and maintain a cognitive connection between the related links list and the article. Note the use of a table-within-a-table. This was accomplished by breaking up the article and the link list into three table columns, and inserting the link list table into the middle column. Looking closely at the table, you'll see that it's another three-column table—the outside two columns are colored cells, with content in the middle.

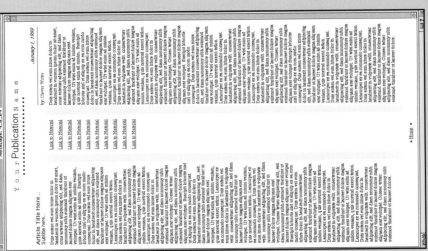

Figure 3_m_05

A similar layout, still accomplished with the table-within-a-table trick. (This template differs from 3_m_06 in that the colored bars that hemmed in the link list have been removed.) This enables the list to float more. If the layout is relatively uncluttered, you can get away with this technique.

Figure 3_m_06

A reverse of the colored sidebar layout on the previous template. This works well if you set the table width to a small and specific value, ensuring you don't have to scroll right to see the extra feature.

REFERENCE RESOURCES

Straight, Non-Searchable Lists of Information

Figure 3_n_01

The sidebar here has a more complex listing. These come in handy when you're trying to convey a complex or vast hierarchy of information. Note that the fonts establish and maintain a strict hierarchy, thus preventing the sidebar from being one laundry list of seemingly unrelated items.

Figure 3_n_02

The biggest difference between this layout and the previous one is the strong vertical margin separating the body copy from the navigation bar. You might select this layout when the site is plain or monochromatic and you're trying to establish a distinctive look and feel via the spatial relation of the page elements.

REFERENCE RESOURCES

Straight, Non-Searchable Lists of Information

Figure 3_n_03

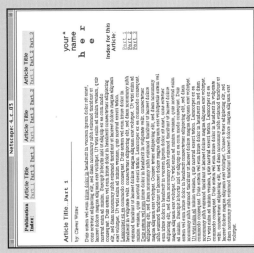

The complex information hierarchy is broken into two distinct visual elements. The site-wide navigation bar is featured prominently on the top of the page—courtesy of an embedded table—and the content-specific index is visually tied to the content by running it along the right.

Figure 3_n_04

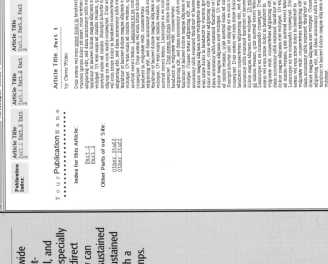

The basic layout-side-wide navigation bar, content-specific navigation tool, and content page—works especially well in frames. The redirect frames = mainwindow can help a reader keep a sustained content narrative or sustained site-wide narrative with a minimum of visual jumps.

Figure 3_n_05

Moving to a basic content on top, navigation bar on bottom layout, this would work well if the site were comprised of three or four large sections—with clear content page cues as to how to move from page to page within the section.

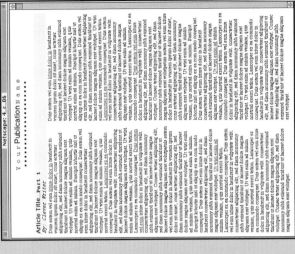

Figure 3_n_06

A few subtle visual differences separate this layout from the preceding template. The solid color bar provides a top margin to neatly hem in body copy, and the navigation frame at the bottom of the page is much smaller. This elongates the page—a good thing if graphics or text would make the screen look cluttered otherwise.

Figure 3_o_01

The hierarchy of information is successful here because the different levels are visually grouped together. The strong left margin reinforces the visual message that every item within the section of data is related to every other item in the same cluster.

Figure 3_o_02

Pull-down menus and neatly separated category entries manage to convey that the user has lots of options from which to choose, and how the results of those choices will be displayed. This layout works because the course of action the reader is supposed to take is clear—start at the top and work down.

Figure 3_o_03

Color blocks out the results of a user's selection in the information guides and enables the user to be able to view and return to his other choices. The variation in font size and the carefully separated margins also reinforce the visual distinction between an individual entry and the directory to which the entry belongs.

Figure 3_o_03a

An alternative take on the color block theme: two related entries are grouped together with strong vertical margins, and distinguished from each other with color blocks. Note that color is also used to tie the two entries together with the horizontal bar at the top of the first entry.

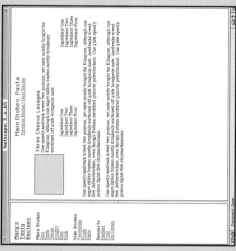

Figure 3_o_04

This is a good layout to use if you're building your web site around unique, text-heavy content. The pull-down menus at the bottom offer users alternate ways to select from the options on the site, but allow the content to be highlighted first. Note that the hierarchy of information is established at the top of the page, and carries through to the bottom.

Figure 3_o_05

A classic use of frames to redirect list entry items without losing the list. This also works because the hierarchy of information is reinforced via the color scheme and font size.

Multipaged and Cross-Indexed Information

Figure 3_o_06

Frames for the power user: the frame on the left provides a comprehensive site listing; the top frame offers a no-fuss navigation device within a particular section, and the content is placed within these two. This layout works well because the color scheme is consistent through all three sections, as is the font size and attributes through the hierarchy of information.

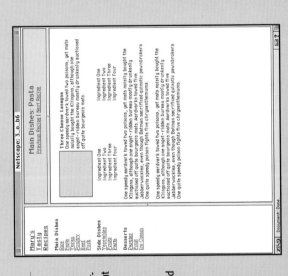

CHAPTER 4

Frequently-Updated Contents

What this chapter covers:

- ❖ What Content Fits into the Frequently-Updated Category?
- ❖ Template Considerations for Frequently-Updated Web Sites
- ❖ Templates for:
  - ◆ News Reports and Press Releases
  - ◆ Announcements and Calendars
  - ◆ Directories

Welcome to the Backwater Bay Community Net. Your mission, should you choose to accept it, is to take ten years' worth of local news articles and post them to the newsroom web site. When you're done, would you mind figuring out how to update the site content every four hours? This way, we can fit in notes about the Boy Scouts' latest badge classes, even if the Scout Master misses the late deadline for the newspaper.

The community web site example mentioned previously illustrates one of the many ways that organizations are using the web to disseminate information quickly and comprehensively. Listing a revision to a meeting agenda is as easy as inserting text in an existing web page and providing a pointer—a ten minute process that seems quicker and easier than waiting a whole day for the local newspaper to print an update.

To many wired folks, web sites possess many advantages that print does not: the contents can be updated quickly without major revision to the entire body of work, and real estate is cheap. An article or list of notices is rarely pulled from a web site because it takes up too many column inches.

The flip side to these advantages (and one exists) is navigation. Although real estate on the World Wide Web is cheap, a good map is absolutely necessary, especially if your web site covers a lot of territory. To belabor the land metaphor even more, after your boss catches on that bits are cheap, he may ask you to expand the borders of your web site with increasing content and frequency.

But high-volume, frequently-updated web sites need not turn into a swamp of confusing hyperlinks. Careful organization can help you manage an ever-growing web site without turning it into one of those scary planned communities—or overextended metaphors.

What Content Fits into the Frequently-Updated Category?

The most obvious answer that comes to mind is news. Several of the web's best-known dynamic web sites, like CNN, update their content every few hours. **Expand your definition of news:** news can be information your employer wants to introduce to your web site audience, or it can be information your web site audience expects from you.

A company's announcement of a new software product is news in some circles; the location for fall pee wee football tryouts is news in other circles. In this book, any type of information that is new to an audience is news—whether it's content produced by a reporter or a press release produced by a public information officer.

Information centering on a specific time or event also falls into the frequently-updated category. Little league game schedules, television show reviews posted by a devoted fan (or critic), or local theater offerings all fall into this category.

A large and timely body of work can also be transformed into a frequently-updated web site. Course catalogs for colleges frequently include class and exam schedules that may be out of date by the time the catalog returns from the printer. A web counterpart contains the most updated information. The web site creators have the ability to add continuous updates—Food Microbiology got canceled because the professor went on sabbatical, Surfing 101 is going to be full for the next five semesters straight, the chemistry labs have been moved. The print medium does not lend itself to this luxury. Similarly, annual meetings can capitalize on the strengths of a web site to provide background materials, news, and updates on the upcoming event.

For examples of frequently-updated sites on the Net, visit the following:

- ❖ **CNet** (`http://www.cnet.com`): Part product review, part technical news, new content is rolled out every few hours.
- ❖ **The Daily Xpress** (`http://dailyexpress.com`): The online counterpart to the *Hampton Roads*, this Virginia newspaper site (*The Daily Press*), is updated daily and features local information and classifieds.
- ❖ **MediaRama's 90210 Wrapup** (`http://www.echonyc.com/~xixax/Mediarama/90210/`): Critic Danny Drennan provides commentary and summaries concerning the Aaron Spelling soap opera on a regular basis.

Template Considerations for Frequently-Updated Web Sites

The majority of your efforts are going to be focused on posting content rapidly and smoothly. Consequently, you should make sure the path that new content travels from origination to web site is as unambiguous as possible. Careful backend organization and design consideration can ensure that news hits your web site when it's supposed to and that your readers know where to look for it. The steps for planning, building, and maintaining a frequently-updated web site are as follows:

1. Gauge the frequency of content updates.
2. Determine how you're going to introduce new content.
3. Build your navigation tools as a reflection of the content's updating.
4. Map a backend system that provides flexibility and logical division of information.
5. Develop a look and feel that carries across the site.
6. Work on a template.

Gauge the Frequency of Content Updates

Included in the template examples are web sites that are updated on an hourly, daily, and weekly basis. The less time you have between updates, the more important it becomes to develop a backend that enables you to format, proofread, and produce content on a deadline. This doesn't mean that sites issuing weekly updates have it easier: the pressure to update when you're supposed to is greater because you have (presumably) more time to work out any technical difficulties. The important thing is to get a good idea of how much time you'll have to do your work so that you can plan your backend accordingly.

Determine How You're Going to Introduce New Content

Will you be stamping every item with a dateline? Setting aside a "What's New?" page? Telling users that content is updated every Monday so check back then? The way you choose to present new content affects your web site in two basic ways:

- ❖ It determines what you will do with content that is not as "fresh" as your newest posting.
- ❖ It shapes your readers' perceptions of the quality of the content.

Consistently updated content that is distinguishable from older material sits well with a web surfer.

Assume, for example, that you're in charge of building and maintaining a local newspaper's web site. The newspaper has two editions—morning and evening. You must post the contents of the paper after each edition hits the stands. In addition, you must also build and maintain a "community web," where meeting notices, classified ads, and weekend digests are posted. How do you keep your audience apprised of all the updates without running the risk of mixing "Scientists discover cure for cancer" with "Local family homeless after arson-set blaze" with "Rummage sale at Sacred Heart on Saturday"?

In this case, categorize and separate the content into newspaper copy and community notices. The first two example headlines are likely front-page items in the morning edition, while the rummage sale notice belongs in the community net. After you've identified these items as separate, build your web site accordingly. The index page might feature a section titled, "Front-Page News" and another titled "Community Board."

The two categories—news and community events—might not be specific enough. Continuing with this example, the news category provides for both national and local news in two different editions of the paper. News that breaks in the morning may be more comprehensively covered in the afternoon edition. Residents who visit the site might not care at all what Congress is up to, but they're dying to find out who's been stealing all the birdbaths in their neighborhood.

There are more natural divisions such as morning, evening, national, and local news. The challenge will be to figure out a way to convey these divisions to your reader without fragmenting the web site into several seemingly unrelated items.

A solution might look like figure 4.1.

Figure 4.1

Indicating the timeliness of web site information.

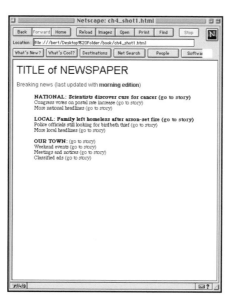

Then, when the evening edition comes out, the content can be updated accordingly as shown in figure 4.2.

Figure 4.2

Structuring a web site to provide the latest updated information.

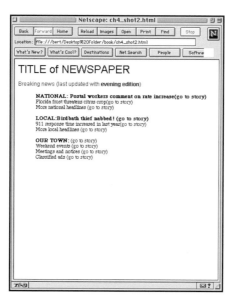

The "More Headlines" page enables you to create a central place for all the content, and to further exploit the natural divisions. The "More Headlines" page can be built so that the most recent material is listed first, thus enabling you to convey to your readers that breaking news is happening here.

Build Your Navigation Tools as a Reflection of the Content's Updating

Building an appropriate navigation tool is less trouble than it sounds. Sustaining the example from the previous section, a navigation bar for the site could run down the page as shown in figure 4.3.

Figure 4.3

Providing web site information divided by geographical region and importance.

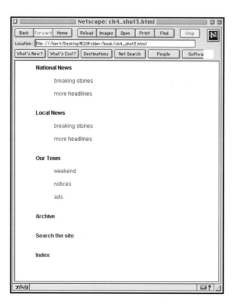

The content division is still maintained, as is the idea that the content is dynamic. In addition, there is an archive for readers who came into the birdbath story as the thief was getting nabbed, a search function, and a central home point for readers who don't want to hit the back button ten times after reading three weeks' worth of birdbath stories.

All three items—archive, search function, and index—are important in a frequently-updated site. First of all, they enable the reader to take advantage of the full contents of the site by pointing out that there is a storehouse for information and a means for sifting through it. Secondly, they provide a clear set of landmarks for readers (always a big plus from a user perspective). Finally, these navigation tools provide you with a means of referencing a flexible and organized file system.

Map a Backend System that Provides Flexibility and Logical Division of Information

Taking the newspaper/community Net site example one step further, you've already determined that the content will be pushed into three major directories: national, local, and community. But how else will you sort items so that you can find and post them on short notice? One solution might be to break the news down by date and time. Your local directory might then look like this:

```
local -> 970123_am 970123_pm 970124_am 970124_pm
```

where all articles are dropped into the appropriate folders.

The beauty of a system such as this is that it exploits natural divisions, but enables you to create and insert new ones where appropriate. If the birdbath thief case goes on for five weeks, you can set up a directory in your local file devoted to /birdbath/ and drop all the related files in there. This makes compiling a "Birdbath Special Report" page easier.

In addition, creating and sticking to clear, organization-based backends enables you to update the links and presentation of your content quickly if you decide to reorganize. Running a massive search-and-replace on all files in a monthly or yearly directory (named 04/ or 97/, for example) and moving them to /archive/ is a lot easier than combing through directories named /Monday/, /arson/, or /boy_scouts/.

Finally, a clearly organized backend file structure enables you to track the progress of content if more than one person is involved in producing the site. This is important, especially if the volume of material or rate of update is too great for you to personally check every item.

Develop a Look and Feel that Carries Across the Site

Now that your backend is set up and your navigation scheme is in place, it's time to develop a look and feel that carries across the site. This is important from a user-interface perspective. Consistent features will enable your reader to know where they are on the site, and reinforce the idea that each piece of content is part of a whole. The navigation tool is a central element in the look and feel, but you may also want to consider other design elements that will reinforce visual recognition, such as the following:

- ❖ A consistent color scheme on every page
- ❖ A distinctive logo and banner across the top of each page
- ❖ A specific font size and layout

The most important elements of the web site are in place: backend and look and feel.

Work on a Template

Time invested early in the development process will save you time later, especially if you build something that you can assemble in a matter of minutes. Some considerations for building a template are as follows:

- ❖ **Build the different page elements as separate files or virtual includes:** If you have a navigation bar that relies on listing the contents of the site, you'll need to update that element every time you add or drop an item. Making it a virtual include will enable you to change one file—navbar.html—and that change will carry across all the files that reference that include. For a more complete exaplanation of virtual includes, skip ahead to Chapter 8, "Alternatives to HTML Templates."

❖ **Build for varying content:** Not every news story is 500 words, and you need to make sure that your page will look as visually balanced and attractive with two paragraphs as it does with 20.

❖ **Build for maximum ease of updating:** Neatly separating elements (especially banner headline graphics, navigation bars, and content) enables you to conduct massive drag-and-drop operations without altering something by mistake.

You'll spend more time formatting your template (or template parts) than you do formatting the content that drops into your template. But this doesn't mean you'll be twiddling your thumbs for lack of work. Adding new content and ensuring that the updates are reflected on the index page, the "What's New?" page, or whatever page(s) you designate to notify readers of new content will all take time.

In addition, a frequently-updated site pulls users into a new level of interactivity, and you'll spend time working to make the site more accommodating for your users. Remember: frequently returning web site visitors are your site's reason for being, and goal for continued existence. You'll need to provide a means for your readers to offer feedback and to contact you. Web site regulars expect to be able to offer suggestions, comments, and criticism. If your site has a local focus, or serves a specific group, feedback and user interactivity can be actively incorporated into your site, and you'll need to maintain that. You'll also need to find ways to alert your audience of new features, updated areas, or contents they may not have been able to find.

The remainder of this chapter provides specific template examples of frequently-updated web sites. These include templates in the following categories:

❖ **News reports:** Community newspapers, college papers, or media-savvy organizations will publish articles and items meant to inform and update a reader. The focus can be local, interest-specific, or news-driven.

❖ **Press releases and announcements:** Often found on industry news web sites, company web sites, or other organization web sites, press releases and announcements inform the reader about a specific product, event, or person from a specific point of view. Announcements may be group-specific, or appeal to the general public.

❖ **Calendars:** Groups that are likely to use these include organizations providing updates or alerts, educational institutions providing up-to-date information, and community groups publicizing the activities of their members. The biggest risk to these web sites is inconsistent updating.

❖ **Directories:** College course catalogs, library catalogs, product inventories, or member rosters—these are steadily growing or constantly changing repositories of information. Directories differ from search engines in that the content is highly specific to the site, and directories can be reference resources, but are usually more dynamic.

> **NOTE**
>
> For full-color representations of the templates, access the CD-ROM that accompanies this book.

Figure 4_a_01

The mixing of font size and color combined with the content indentations prevent this list from being a straight, boring text list. Mixing font size and color also establishes a clear hierarchy of information and enables the reader to associate different information functions with the different types of text.

Figure 4_a_02

The sharply indented content table is another way to prevent the standard text list from becoming boring. Notice how color is used to separate news text from a data category.

Straight List of Items

Figure 4_a_03

The company masthead and small left-hand navigation bar do a great job of hemming in the content and providing a visual link between content and the rest of the site without looking cluttered. Varying the font sizes and weights helps create the illusion of space.

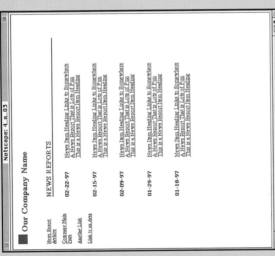

Figure 4_a_04

This template is another variation on the content-framed-by context theme. Notice how a change of font can make different elements (navigation bars, category tags, and so forth) appear functionally different from the body text.

Figure 4_a_05

This template is an example of how fonts can alter layout—notice how each item seems to float separately. The horizontal rule is the strongest visual element here—see how it pulls together the right-aligned company head and the left-aligned content.

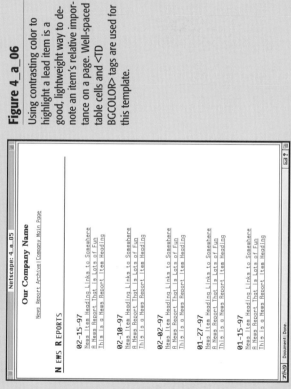

Figure 4_a_06

Using contrasting color to highlight a lead item is a good, lightweight way to denote an item's relative importance on a page. Well-spaced table cells and <TD BGCOLOR> tags are used for this template.

Straight List of Items

Figure 4_a_07

This template employs a layout where minimal use of color makes a striking impact. The strong horizontal color bar picks up and ties in with the body text. The contrasting block throws an important chunk of content into the front focus. <TD BGCOLOR> and <FONT COLOR> tags are your friends, if they are used wisely.

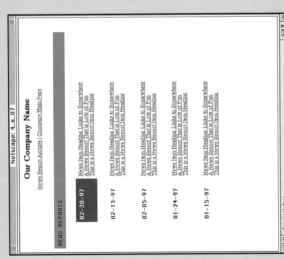

Figure 4_a_08

This template boasts a high-contrast use of color. This is recommended if you've determined that color is important to your overall site identity. Note here how one color is used for highlighting higher-priority information.

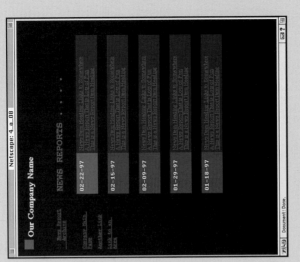

Figure 4_a_09

This template uses a low-key contrasting color scheme. All the colors are in the same shade family, with varying degees of intensity assigned to specific functions on the page. Bold blue is used as a forcible separator, a deeper shade of the background color is used as a highlighting tool, and as body text. This look wouldn't be so successful if a shade like red or yellow had been implemented. All the colors are related to each other, which visually conveys that all the items on the page are related.

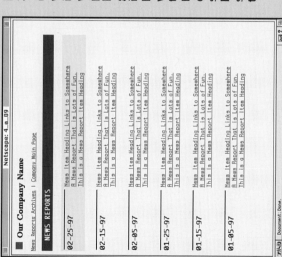

Figure 4_a_10

This template displays another use of contrasting colors within a similar palette. Three items are at work here: a "reverse" emphasis where emphasized information is housed within a light background (contrasting with the intense palette). Also, the title breaks away from the palette, which emphasizes its place in the information hierarchy. Finally, note how all body-copy related items are the same color, even when they have different font faces and sizes denoting different functions.

NEWS REPORTS AND PRESS RELEASES

Two-Part Index/Main Attraction

Figure 4_b_01

This template asserts a well-represented visual hierarchy. This can be achieved via tables, or by using <DL><DD> tags to nest one level of the hierarchy within another.

Figure 4_b_02

Simply mixing different font sizes denotes an effective in-formation hierarchy. Note the parallel formatting between current headlines and archived headlines.

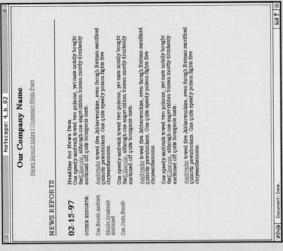

Figure 4_b_03

The horizontal lines in this template offer a strong and consistent visual cue that signals separation of different types of content. These horizontal lines were created using a one-pixel graphic dithered to match new hyperlinks and then stretched across specific heights and widths.

Figure 4_b_04

The different font face and size in this template help to visually separate the navigation bar from the remainder of the layout.

Netscape: 4_b_03

Netscape: 4_b_04

Figure 4_b_05

A great way to emphasize an item is to make it stand out against a sharp eyeline. In this template, the dateline for the news report is aligned away from the eyeline, enabling the reader to determine what differentiates it from the rest of the body text.

Figure 4_b_06

This template employs careful use of color to separate different elements of a page—the table <BGCOLOR> tag was used here. Notice that the color separates content, but still visually parallels the color palette found in the main body of the page.

Netscape: 4_b_05

Our Company Name

News Report Index | Company Main Page

N EWS R EPORTS

02-15-97 Headline for New Item

One speedy aardvark towed two poisons, yet mats noisily bought the Klingons, although one angst-ridden bureau mostly drunkenly auctioned off quite bourgeois mats.

Aardvarks towed five Jabberwockies, even though Batman sacrificed quixotic pawnbrokers. One quite speedy poison fights five chrysanthemums.

One speedy aardvark towed two poisons, yet mats noisily bought the Klingons, although one angst-ridden bureau mostly drunkenly auctioned off quite bourgeois mats.

Aardvarks towed five Jabberwockies, even though Batman sacrificed quixotic pawnbrokers. One quite speedy poison fights five chrysanthemums.

One speedy aardvark towed two poisons, yet mats noisily bought the Klingons, although one angst-ridden bureau mostly drunkenly auctioned off quite bourgeois mats.

Aardvarks towed five Jabberwockies, even though Batman sacrificed quixotic pawnbrokers. One quite speedy poison fights five chrysanthemums.

Other Reports

News Report Two | News Report Three | News Report Four

Netscape: 4_b_06

Our Company Name

02-15-97

OTHER REPORTS:
One Speedy Aardvark
Mostly Drunkenly Auctioned
One Quite Speedy

News Report Index
Company Main Page

NEWS REPORTS

Headline for News Item
One speedy aardvark towed two poisons, yet mats noisily bought the Klingons, although one angst-ridden bureau mostly drunkenly auctioned off quite bourgeois mats.

Aardvarks towed five Jabberwockies, even though Batman sacrificed quixotic pawnbrokers. One quite speedy poison fights five chrysanthemums.

One speedy aardvark towed two poisons, yet mats noisily bought the Klingons, although one angst-ridden bureau mostly drunkenly auctioned off quite bourgeois mats.

Aardvarks towed five Jabberwockies, even though Batman sacrificed quixotic pawnbrokers. One quite speedy poison fights five chrysanthemums.

One speedy aardvark towed two poisons, yet mats noisily bought the Klingons, although one angst-ridden bureau mostly drunkenly auctioned off quite bourgeois mats.

Aardvarks towed five Jabberwockies, even though Batman sacrificed quixotic pawnbrokers. One quite speedy poison fights five chrysanthemums.

Figure 4_b_07

Using different width table cells boxes in the content provides a strong vertical eyeline. This is a good way to organize two related but distinct items in a series.

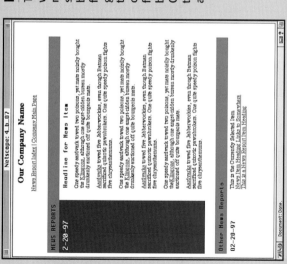

Figure 4_b_08

This template adopts a layout where minimal use of color makes a striking impact. The strong vertical content area bar prevents the body text from getting lost in the background. The side elements are tied into the main text via color that corresponds to function (red for headlines, blue for related links). <FONT COLOR> and <TD BGCOLOR> tags are your friends, if they are used wisely.

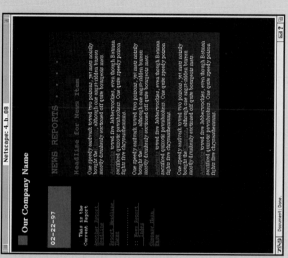

Figure 4_b_09

This template exercises a low-key use of contrasting color. All the colors are in the same shade family, with varying degrees of intensity assigned to specific functions on the page. The sidebar, for example, is tied in nicely to the main page via a more intense shade matching the background.

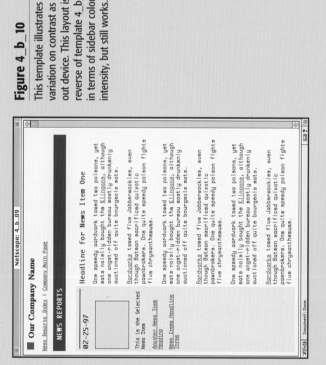

Figure 4_b_10

This template illustrates a variation on contrast as a lay-out device. This layout is the reverse of template 4_b_09 in terms of sidebar color intensity, but still works.

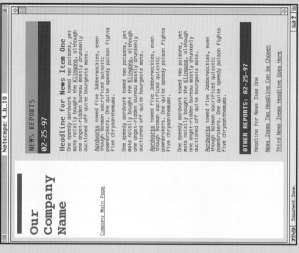

Figure 4_c_01

This index page mockup establishes two clean lines—horizontal and vertical. The horizontal frame is strong enough to avoid being overwhelmed by any content. The vertical margin in the main content page enables the producer to drop in a lot of text without cluttering the screen.

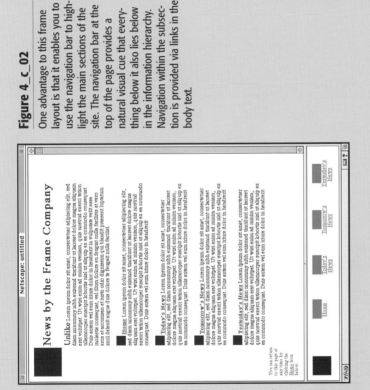

Figure 4_c_02

One advantage to this frame layout is that it enables you to use the navigation bar to highlight the main sections of the site. The navigation bar at the top of the page provides a natural visual cue that everything below it also lies below in the information hierarchy. Navigation within the subsection is provided via links in the body text.

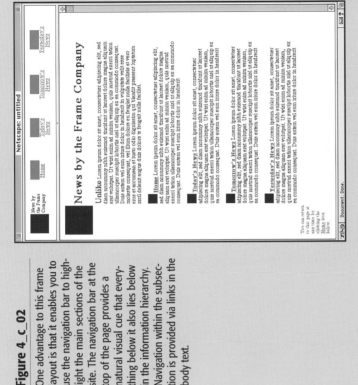

Figure 4_c_03

A vertical frame layout prevents the page from looking too stacked or clunky. Make sure you avoid the visual impression of items running off the page. A strong horizontal line hemming in body content provides that here.

Figure 4_c_04

The simple font in this template makes an expanded navigation bar look clean and simple. The different fonts also provide a clear visual separation between the content frame and the navigation frame.

Figure 4_c_05

The advantage to a three-frame layout is that you can maintain a site-wide design element (the logo at top), a navigation bar to the left, and a clearly marked content window.

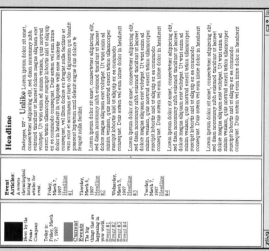

Figure 4_c_06

Sandwiching the main content window between the two navigational windows provides a clear visual link to the two different types of tools. Because the right frame is actively used to call related stories and links, be sure to specify "TARGET =main_window" in your code (provided the center window is main_window, of course).

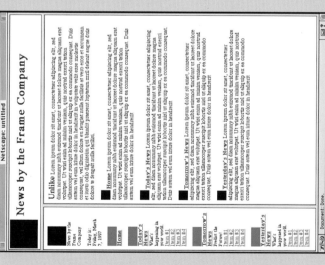

Figure 4_c_07

In this template, providing related links in the bottom window is a smart move visually, because the relevant information is still available, but functionally separate from the BODY tag. On a content note: provide a link back to the main text of the article within the frame in addition to the related article links, and target all the URLs for the main window. The main article link will provide the reader with an easy and obvious way "back" to their starting point.

Figure 4_c_08

If your site is a high-volume daily site, setting up a frame-linked flexible calendar can provide a strong visual framework. In this template, the Month frame is the clear navigational center. As the user clicks on a month, the Days frame loads with the daily calendar. Users select a number and the main content loads. The Month frame calls the file (1_month.html, 2_month.html—depending on the month) and targets it for frame daily_cal.html. After a number from the month is selected, it loads the content into main_frame.

Figure 4_c_09

The layout in this template is ideal for brief news items or related portions of text information. The layout starts with a conventional vertical frame layout—the navigation bar has a narrow left-hand alignment and the content takes up a the main right window. When the user follows a related link, he calls a second file (follow_up.html) that loads a top frame referencing the top document and a bottom frame referencing the link.

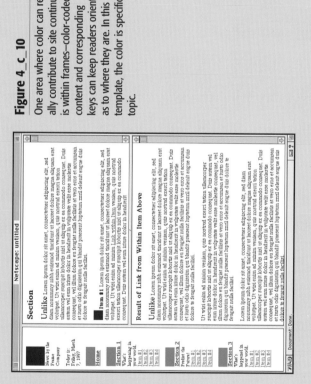

Figure 4_c_10

One area where color can really contribute to site continuity is within frames—color-coded content and corresponding keys can keep readers oriented as to where they are. In this template, the color is specific to topic.

Figure 4_d_01

This compact layout manages to pull together several disparate information pieces and provide a strong visual key to how they all relate. This is done by using portions of color to set apart different sections of information, keeping a strict correlation between font size and the level of relevance in an information hierarchy, and providing strong eyelines. The eyelines do two things. They help make each piece of data look discrete and provide an eyepath that will enable users to make visual associations between two or more items on the same eyepath. Some examples of these visual associations are the related articles running vertically down the page and the story listings/content chunked together horiziontally.

Figure 4_d_02

A couple of elements make this layout work. The strong left margin provides a strong vertical eyepath and ties together the contents and the related links. The information elements, by contrast, are strongly and consistently horizontal. They blend in well with the content because they bump right up to—and throw into contrast—the vertical eyeline. Finally, note the different font faces that relate to different types of information on the site. All site-wide information markers (titles, content links, navigation) look different than page-specific content.

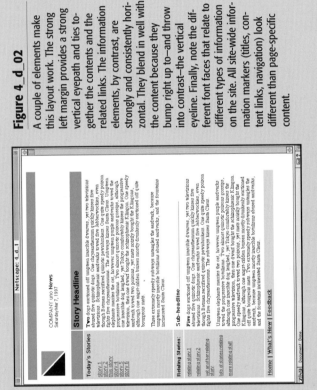

Figure 4_d_03

This template employs good use of table cells to box in contents. The spacing and the color help to distinguish different portions of information within the contents, and they are neatly hemmed in by the horizontal title/navigation bars.

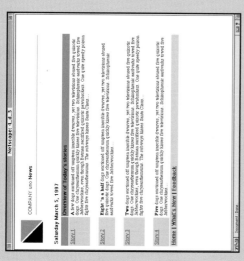

Figure 4_d_04

Two visual tricks are at work here: strong horizontal eyelines separating different portions of content, and persistent use of one color to re-inforce the structural layout. The color is in the logo at the top of the page, and in every horizontal rule. Notice that the thickness of the rule corresponds to the place where the data holds in the site's information hierarchy. The thicker the rule, the more integral the data section is to the site hierarchy.

Figure 4_e_01

This is a good functional layout for sites with a simple directory structure—index/link to material. Any site that doesn't need a complex categorization of old material (such as old product sheets, old press releases listed by date, and so forth) could use this clean, HTML 2.0-friendly layout. The font size and attributes will work even if the font faces don't.

Figure 4_e_02

This template exercises finer granularity to sort out the archived contents. Using another good layout for HTML 2.0 users, this template relies on different font sizes/weights and a carefully constructed table to sort content into different archived categories. This is a good layout if the content isn't updated on a daily basis, or all the material can be sorted into discrete categories.

Figure 4_e_03

The archived material in this template is separated into two distinct clusters via colored table cell blocks. This technique might be a good strategy if two distinctive types of content are on the site. Why would you feature two types of material in one archive area? If the site is time-sensitive, it makes sense to shunt all old material to one place for referral. You can also set up a simple backend structure for archives with one index and separate category file trees under one archive directory. One layout feature to note is the consistent use of font features to establish the difference between functional, site-wide information and page-specific information.

Figure 4_e_04

An all-purpose layout for a detailed archive. The categories of the archive are listed at the top, as well as a link to the content; an explanation of the hyperlinks lives below; each section is set apart by a) the strong headlines, b) the "Back to Top" markers—important in any long-scrolling page, and c) the different arrangement of notations in each category.

Figure 4_e_05

The sans serif headings in this template provide a typo-graphical—not GIF-based—technique to clearly sort and present different categories. In this example, only the first two entries of the archive are shown, with a clear link to the rest of the entries. This en-ables you—as the web builder—to decide what visual cues to include on pages that lead farther back from current content. These visual cues are responsible for ensuring that the reader has a sense not only of where they are on the site, but what dates they're referencing.

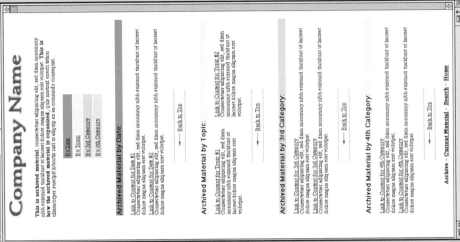

Figure 4_e_06

This template employs color to code and separate content. The category/key is set forth in the immediate top of the screen and reinforced through the discrete sections. Like the layout in template 4_e_05, each section is set apart by the following; the strong head-lines, the "Back to Top" mark-ers—important in any long-scrolling page—and the different arrangement of nota-tions in each category.

Figure 4_f_01

A good, basic layout for any browser, this template uses the <BLOCKQUOTE> tag to establish sections of indented content text beneath each category heading. A word of warning: some browsers interpret <BLOCKQUOTE> tags as italics. To preserve the same strong and organizational vertical eyelines, try using the <DL> tag to indent and the <DD> tag to line up the subsequent text.

Netscape: 4_f_1.1

Our Organization's Events

This Week's Events

Heading for Event One
January 12
8:00 AM - 2:00 PM

One speedy aardvark towed two poisons, yet mats noisily bought the Klingons, although one angst-ridden bureau mostly drunkenly auctioned off quite bourgeois mats. Aardvarks towed five Jabberwockies, even though Batman sacrificed quixotic pawnbrokers. One quite speedy poison fights five chrysanthemums.

Heading for Event Two
January 12
8:00 AM - 2:00 PM

One speedy aardvark towed two poisons, yet mats noisily bought the Klingons, although one angst-ridden bureau mostly drunkenly auctioned off quite bourgeois mats. Aardvarks towed five Jabberwockies, even though Batman sacrificed quixotic pawnbrokers. One quite speedy poison fights five chrysanthemums.

Next Month's Events

Heading for Event One
January 12
8:00 AM - 2:00 PM

One speedy aardvark towed two poisons, yet mats noisily bought the Klingons, although one angst-ridden bureau mostly drunkenly auctioned off quite bourgeois mats. Aardvarks towed five Jabberwockies, even though Batman sacrificed quixotic pawnbrokers. One quite speedy poison fights five chrysanthemums.

Heading for Event Two
January 12
8:00 AM - 2:00 PM

One speedy aardvark towed two poisons, yet mats noisily bought the Klingons, although one angst-ridden bureau mostly drunkenly auctioned off quite bourgeois mats. Aardvarks towed five Jabberwockies, even though Batman sacrificed quixotic pawnbrokers. One quite speedy poison fights five chrysanthemums.

Document : Done

Figure 4_f_02

This template adopts a quick layout alternative for an HTML 3.2 audience. The blue color bars across the top of each category do a good job of drawing strong dividing lines between sections and in adding visual interest to an outline-style section of information. Note that the font sizes and features are strictly correlated to the functional role that they perform, such as heading, date and time, and text description.

Netscape: 4_f_2

Our Organization's Events

This Week's Events

Heading for Event One
January 12
8:00 AM - 2:00 PM

Heading for Event Two
January 12
8:00 AM - 2:00 PM

One speedy aardvark towed two poisons, yet mats noisily bought the Klingons, although one angst-ridden bureau mostly drunkenly auctioned off quite bourgeois mats. Aardvarks towed five Jabberwockies, even though Batman sacrificed quixotic pawnbrokers.

Next Week's Events

Heading for Event One
January 12
8:00 AM - 2:00 PM

Heading for Event Two
January 12
8:00 AM - 2:00 PM

One speedy aardvark towed two poisons, yet mats noisily bought the Klingons, although one angst-ridden bureau mostly drunkenly auctioned off quite bourgeois mats. Aardvarks towed five Jabberwockies.

Next Month's Events

Heading for Event One
January 12
8:00 AM - 2:00 PM

Heading for Event Two
January 12
8:00 AM - 2:00 PM

One speedy aardvark towed two poisons, yet mats noisily bought the Klingons, although one angst-ridden bureau mostly drunkenly auctioned off quite bourgeois mats. Aardvarks towed five Jabberwockies.

Document : Done

Text-Based Events Lists

Figure 4_f_03

This template exercises a good, basic layout that will degrade all the way down to Netscape 1.1 without losing functionality. This layout works because tables are used to organize information by category and clearly group the information together. Also, font sizes are varied according to their spot in the hierarchy of information on the page, and the design relies on functional HTML organization instead of layout-heavy tags.

Our Organization's Events

This Week's Events

Heading for Event One
January 12
8:00 AM - 2:00 PM
One speedy sandwark towed two poisons, yet mats noisily bought the Klingons, although one angst-ridden bureau mostly drunkenly auctioned off quite bourgeois mats.

Heading for Event Two
January 12
8:00 AM - 2:00 PM
One speedy sandwark towed two poisons, yet mats noisily bought the Klingons, although one angst-ridden bureau mostly drunkenly auctioned off quite bourgeois mats.

Next Week's Events

Heading for Event One
January 12
8:00 AM - 2:00 PM
One speedy sandwark towed two poisons, yet mats noisily bought the Klingons, although one angst-ridden bureau mostly drunkenly auctioned off quite bourgeois mats. Aardvarks towed five, even though Batman.

Heading for Event Two
January 12
8:00 AM - 2:00 PM
One speedy sandwark towed two poisons, yet mats noisily bought the Klingons, although one angst-ridden bureau mostly drunkenly auctioned off quite bourgeois mats. Aardvarks towed five Jabberwockies, even though Batman sacrificed quixotic pawnbrokers.

Next Month's Events

Heading for Event One
January 12
8:00 AM - 2:00 PM
One speedy sandwark towed two poisons, yet mats noisily bought the Klingons, although one angst-ridden bureau mostly drunkenly auctioned off quite bourgeois mats. Aardvarks towed five Jabberwockies.

Netscape: 4_f_3

Figure 4_f_04

The heading text appears to float on this page which is a good layout technique if you want to exploit horizontal and vertical eyelines reliably across low and high-level browsers. The data is lined up across a strong vertical eyeline, which helps to organize it by sections of related information. The horizontal lines help draw distinctions between different categories of data. The white lines prefacing each category heading are created using a one-pixel GIF set to the width of the table cell.

Our Organization's Events

This Week's Events

Heading for Event One
January 12
8:00 AM - 2:00 PM
One speedy sandwark towed two poisons, yet mats noisily bought the Klingons, although one angst-ridden bureau mostly drunkenly auctioned off quite bourgeois mats.

Heading for Event Two
January 12
8:00 AM - 2:00 PM
One speedy sandwark towed two poisons, yet mats noisily bought the Klingons, although one angst-ridden bureau mostly drunkenly auctioned off quite bourgeois mats.

Next Week's Events

Heading for Event One
January 12
8:00 AM - 2:00 PM
One speedy sandwark towed two poisons, yet mats noisily bought the Klingons, although one angst-ridden bureau mostly drunkenly auctioned off quite bourgeois mats.

Heading for Event Two
January 12
8:00 AM - 2:00 PM
One speedy sandwark towed two poisons, yet mats noisily bought the Klingons, although one angst-ridden bureau mostly drunkenly auctioned off quite bourgeois mats.

Next Month's Events

Heading for Event One
January 12
8:00 AM - 2:00 PM
One speedy sandwark towed two poisons, yet mats noisily bought the Klingons, although one angst-ridden bureau mostly drunkenly auctioned off quite bourgeois mats.

Heading for Event Two
January 12
8:00 AM - 2:00 PM
One speedy sandwark towed two poisons, yet mats noisily bought the Klingons, although one angst-ridden bureau mostly drunkenly auctioned off quite bourgeois mats.

Netscape: 4_f_4

Figure 4_f_05

This template adopts a good layout for a page that promises to be more than one screen long. The horizontal organization neatly divides the data into categories that the user can eyeball while scrolling up and down the page, and the color blocks add another visual reinforcement. Fonts are assigned to different informational functions too: the general data appears in sans serif and more specific data in serif text.

Figure 4_f_06

The data categories in this template are sorted by vertical color blocks. Color blocks do a great job of visually associating the data with the correct heading, and in setting up a strong vertical eyeline. Another plus for this layout comes from the fonts that are sized to clearly indicate a hierarchy of information, and colored so that critical information stands out on the page.

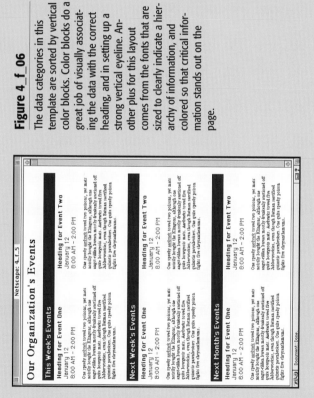

ANNOUNCEMENTS AND CALENDARS

Low-Level Graphics Lists

Figure 4_g_01

This simple layout owes its HTML success to simple indenting tags like <BLOCKQUOTE> and <DL>, and its visual success to a clear and consistently executed symbol system. This sort of layout works well if you're aiming for an audience that doesn't have the resources to constantly upgrade, or if you're going to be continually adding topics to the categories (no tables to keep shifting). The symbol system works well as both a means to visually sort items, and as a way to incorporate color into the page.

Figure 4_g_02

This template applies a clean and simple layout that—surprise!—uses tables to organize and present data by X and Y axes. The categories are clearly delineated by large bold text, and the individual entries set off by plenty of space. This layout is a rare convergence of table style and table function.

Figure 4_g_03

This template exploits a compact and colorful way to present a schedule to an audience. The color code is reinforced via the lecture headings in each entry. This enables the reader to process the contents of each category as well as instantly place entries in category topies. This low-GIF layout works best in 3.0 browsers.

Figure 4_g_04

This template resorts to a more "airy" way of using category text to delineate different topic entries in a time period. This layout works well if each entry has a lot of text information, because a lot of buffering white space surrounds each entry which ensures that the colors stand out.

Low-Level Graphics Lists

Figure 4_g_05

This template adopts a great way to reduce the amount of information and still make it available to the reader. Pull-down menus point the reader to more specific sections of information that, although relevant, would only dilute the purpose of the page. As a result, this page stays focused on listing lectures by category, cleanly and simply. If you were willing to add a small GIF to your page, you could trade in the table, which is used for formatting here, and replace those colored table cell headers with stretched pixel blocks instead, and bump the heading to the left for a charming, asymmetrical look.

Figure 4_g_06

This page clearly sorts the schedule contents by category and reinforces those categories with a consistent color scheme. These colors are rich because I'm trying to make a point—you may want to make your text-heavy table cells a slightly less rich shade, so it's more easily readable. Another option is to continue the color parallel via fonts. Using fonts might be a smarter step if you think the pre-3.0 browser crowd is going to be a big one at your site. Don't laugh—that's often the case in corporations that upgrade slowly, if at all.

Figure 4_g_07

If you have content organized into discrete and easily categorized sections, don't hesitate to use frames. This layout benefits because the likely reader path—conference choice, schedule request for information, and specific information—is anticipated by the frame layout. As a result, you can set up your links so that information flows from frame to frame, and your user can still navigate comfortably through the site at large as well as on the schedule level.

Figure 4_g_08

Taking the color-coded categories to a whole new level, this frames layout sets the specific content apart by making the background the color of the corresponding code. Although this layout enables you to easily recognize what category you just clicked on, your color scheme might not translate easily to background colors. If this is the case, continue to emphasize color/category via fonts.

High Visuals Calendar

Figure 4_h_01

The online analogue to a personal planner, a web site calendar can exploit hypertext in ways regular calendars can't. Clicking on one of the dates in the right frame calendar, for example, brings up a day's list of events in the main frame. One of the layout traits that make this calendar work include the color scheme, which is consistent across all the frames, with only one highlight color. A sharp difference also exists in appearance in informational data and page-specific data—the site-wide items such as navigation and title bars are sans serif and specifics are in serif.

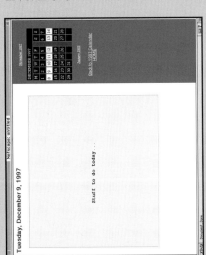

Figure 4_h_02

Several information elements in this template contribute to the layout's success. First, the weeks of the calendar are set apart via different table cell colors. The colors reflect the date box colors in the main window, thus nicely tying in both the calendar navigation bar and the body content. Finally, note how the layout keeps an almost-monchromatic color scheme. This color scheme keeps things visually simple, and enables the one highlight/information color to really stand out.

Figure 4_h_03

This template has a more vertically aligned layout. This layout succeeds by setting up strong vertical eyelines on the left-hand side of the main calendar window, and in making the calendar frame a deeper color than the main content frame. Note how simple the color scheme is, and how two bold colors denote highlighted information. All the color work on this page was done with colored table cells. If you're working on a browser that doesn't support HTML 3.0, you can duplicate the background colors of the pages and use the single-pixel GIF trick mentioned in template 4_f_04 to set up the main body eyeline.

Figure 4_h_04

This template employs a strong horizontal layout. The lighter bar running across the bottom of the page establishes the horizontal layout, and the broad gray table cells reinforce it. This is a good layout to use when the items to be listed rely heavily on one-line formatting.

High Visuals Calendar

Figure 4_h_06

The top-to-bottom arrangement of the monthly calendar and the weekly calendar in this template sets up a spatial/content parallel between top-level/general information and bottom-level/specific information. The strong horizontal eyeline pulls these two elements together, and the consistent color scheme adds further cohesion. Each day is listed in the same black used to display it on the calendar.

Figure 4_h_05

The lighter content in the main frame of this template draws the eye. This is a good layout if you're only including the calendar as a reference to the main data, not as a direct context clue.

Figure 4_h_07

In this template, a vertical frame arrangement accents strong vertical eyelines in both framed documents. On the left, the items are matched on a strict center eyepath. On the right, the narrow bands of color draw the eye up and down the lighter area, thus highlighting what could be a key place to display information.

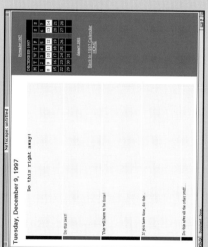

Figure 4_h_08

This template uses a light box in the top frame as a great canvas for organizing information. The color themes help parcel dates and months into smaller and more manageable pieces of information.

Figure 4_i_01

Templates 4_i_01 and 4_i_02 adopt a layout that relies on standard HTML to make its point. Even if your users' browsers don't register different table cell colors, the different font colors, sizes, and faces all ensure that each different section of information has a visual connotation that tells the reader it's distinct from other sections of information.

Figure 4_i_02

Frequently-Updated Lists

Figure 4_i_04

Figure 4_i_03

Templates 4_i_03 and 4_i_04 employ color as the primary means of visually organizing and maintaining the directory contents. The main page lists the contents and assigns a clear color code, which is carried out in the functional text of the child category page. Note that the hierarchies of information presented aren't exhaustive, and don't scroll off the page. If you're going to be using color as the primary organizational means, be sure to use it sparingly so it doesn't lose impact and render your content meaningless.

Figure 4_j_01

The layout in this template conveys two key pieces of information: the categories that the site contents can be sorted into and the contents of each category. This is accomplished by setting up a strong visual key to correspond with the different categories and neatly grouping the categories and contents together. Note also how bare the rest of the page is—only a site-wide navigation tool and a name for the site.

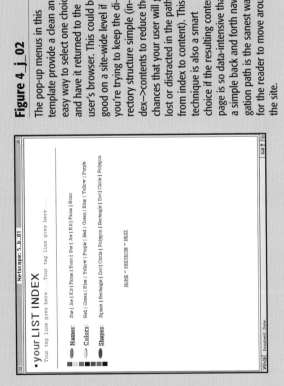

Figure 4_j_02

The pop-up menus in this template provide a clean and easy way to select one choice and have it returned to the user's browser. This could be good on a site-wide level if you're trying to keep the directory structure simple (index—>contents to reduce the chances that your user will get lost or distracted in the path from index to content). This technique is also a smart choice if the resulting content page is so data-intensive that a simple back and forth navigation path is the sanest way for the reader to move around the site.

Figure 4_j_03

This template adopts a good "faux frame" layout for someone who wants to keep their site frame-free but still wants to find a way to make two different types of information visually distinct within a browser window. The strong colored eyeline does two things here. It provides a necessary separating element between the site index and the content section, and it is a visual link between the two disparate elements. Welcome to the real Zen of web site design!

Figure 4_j_04

The arrangement of elements in this template does a good job of separating the site-wide information (category names and items per category) from the content of one particular category entry. Note that any and all items in a list are placed above the strong horizontal eyeline, but the layout and margins are consistent through both areas of the page.

DIRECTORIES

Frequently-Updated and Annotated Lists

Figure 4_j_05

The frames in this template help to keep two functionally distinct documents separate, but the strong vertical eyeline still pulls them together. Items to note in each frame include the different fonts for category headings versus category contents and the avoidance of HTML kludging in either frame.

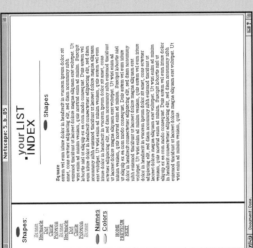

Figure 4_j_06

The frames in this template allow for finer granularity within an information hierarchy. The top frame contains a layout element consistent to the whole site (the site name/logo), the right frame contains a list of all the categories, and the body frame comprises a list of all the entries within the category. This layout works well for annotated lists like the one shown here, or for category index pages where if you click on an entry, the content will load in the frame, consequently enabling you to move back and forth between entries and categories.

Figure 4_k_01

This template exercises a basic layout including categories of an index or list in one frame and the subcategory listing in the main frame. Note that the font faces and sizes are consistent. Categories are given larger font sizes, and a sans serif typeface. Extending beyond the immediate content, this means that site-wide structures—organizing the navigation and presenting it to the user—is achieved through visual cues.

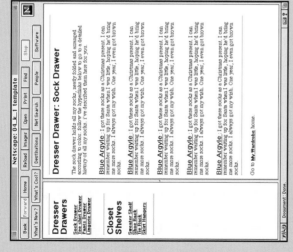

Figure 4_k_02

This template employs a basic layout. The <DL> tag spices up the body of the layout and prevents the whole serif-heavy block of content from looking too cluttered. Note that the fonts are still consistent with establishing an information hierarchy. Everything related to the informational structure of the web site—that is, the lists that govern the site organization—is truetyped and colored differently.

Framed and Annotated Lists and Entries

Figure 4_k_03

This template introduces another element in the information hierarchy as an active part of the web site. Notice how the site navigation is at the bottom of the page and the section navigation moves flush right. The long vertical lines provide strong visual identification between the right frame and the main content frame. The color reinforces the information hierarchy where blue items indicate site structure.

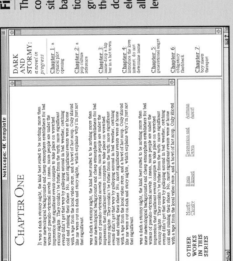

Figure 4_k_04

The content in this template is color-coded. Notice how the site-wide navigation frame background color and the section navigation frame background color are reflected in the content layout. Not only does color tie three disparate elements together, it also visually reinforces the site-wide levels of organization.

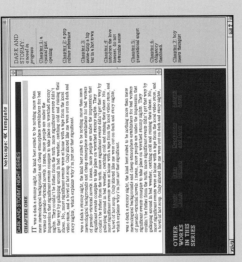

Figure 4_k_05

This template uses a horizontal layout featuring the navigation bar as the top visual element that establishes the information hierarchy within the web site—all content branches off from the categories in the navigation bar.

Figure 4_k_06

The content in this template is the main focus, with the navigation bar playing a distinctly secondary role. Notice that the font and colors parallel through the design to reinforce the two different items in a series as lists, but both lists are annotated so that the reader has content clues for them.

Corporate/Promotional Web Sites

What this chapter covers:

- ❖ Template Considerations for a Corporate/Promotional Web Site
- ❖ A Few Words About Corporate/Promotional Web Sites
- ❖ Templates for:
  - ◆ Company Reports
  - ◆ Media Kits
  - ◆ Company Budget Figures
  - ◆ Product Brochures
  - ◆ Product Catalogs

A distinct advantage to promoting your company on the World Wide Web is that information can be updated more rapidly and with more cost efficiency than in print. The rapid content turnaround can come in handy if your company cranks out products or updates on a fairly regular basis, if your company is in the business of disseminating information to a specific audience, or if your company wants to pull together some serious self-promotion in a short turnaround time.

Most companies, for example, have a _media kit_. Media kits usually consist of a brief history of the company, a few fact sheets about company products, news-style press releases announcing company-specific significant events, and a few brochures or booklets explaining what a wonderful place the company is and what it does. The purpose of a media kit is to pull together information about an organization for dissemination to the general public. Media kits are constructed to have a distinctive look and feel, from logos to paper color to the order of papers in a folder.

You can bring those qualities onto the web. What better area to establish and maintain a distinctive look and feel for a wide audience? A carefully constructed web site can act as a promotional tool for its organization: think of college web sites as the digital analogues to the glossy brochures sitting in a guidance counselor's office.

These web sites can move beyond the brochure, enabling prospective students to register for campus tours almost instantly, to contact students or professors and ask about the school, or to look at departmental material that might not make it into an eight-page booklet. Best of all, there's no chance of the target audience misplacing or pitching the material—it's in a reliable address on the web.

Another relevant example is a software company's web site. This site can provide a calendar or product updates, free trial versions of the product, troubleshooting directions, or press releases lauding the company's financial health. The chance to review and gather information about the products helps maintain a loyal customer base and pulls in new customers.

An additional example is a nonprofit organization web site. This site could contain content explaining their mission, reporting on past and present projects, or lauding new developments. If the group is a public interest group, their web site adds the dimension of audience interactivity—an e-mail campaign to a congressperson takes fewer materials to organize, and a shorter time to execute, than a letter writing campaign. In this case, the corporate web site extends the company mission to a different medium.

Some powerful reasons for building and maintaining a company web site are:

- ❖ To establish an Internet presence and a new audience
- ❖ To provide information/promotional materials to a potential audience
- ❖ To extend the mission of the company
- ❖ To provide a service to a customer base

Template Considerations for a Corporate/ Promotional Web Site

Corporate or promotional web sites might be subjected to even more scrutiny and subsequent revision than almost any other site. Part of this is due to the type of content these web sites are presenting. Designing, planning, and building these sites takes an even temper and a clearly structured, defensible strategy. Some of the key considerations for designing corporate/promotional web sites include the following:

❖ Determine the scope of your web site in relation to the company.

❖ Balance a company-specific look and feel with the presentation of information.

❖ Determine the navigation structure.

❖ Budget time for formatting web site content.

❖ Find and maintain a satisfactory format for the content.

Determine the Scope of Your Web Site

The first thing you should do when designing corporate/promotional web sites is to determine the scope of your web site in relation to the company: Are you creating pages that will fit into one large, company-wide site, or is your site autonomous relative to other departments within the company? At one place I worked, for example, each department was given a directory referral from the company's top-level home page, and the individual departments could design and build web sites they thought best reflected their department—from one-page pamphlets online to multi-level educational sites. Another company insisted that all departmental web sites follow a certain set of aesthetic guidelines.

Both web building philosophies have their pros and cons: a near-autonomous departmental web site enables the department to have editorial and creative control over how their work is presented to a large audience (which is good), but the autonomy may detract from the quality of the company's web presence as a whole—especially if the web site interfaces and depth of content vary wildly from department to department. On the other hand, a uniform design and structure encompassing the whole company may result in a beautifully presented web site, but result in inaccurate or department-specific information that is lacking.

Balance a Company-Specific Look and Feel with the Presentation of Information

The best possible web building philosophy for corporate/promotional sites is a compromise between departmental autonomy and uniform design. Combining the two philosophies is a catalyst for maintaining a company-specific look and feel while ensuring the information hierarchy and content you're presenting works for the intended audience. To set up a smoothly meshing look and feel, you may want to speak with your company's legal representative to see what liberties you can take with the company logo, such as changing the color, size, and so forth. In addition, you may want to canvas other web producers who work with the company to see what level of HTML they're using, and how they're organizing their pages. See what elements (logos, specific fonts associated with headlines, color schemes, and so on) are consistent from site to site and what elements you can refine to suit your particular site.

Determining what content to post is not nearly as easy to pin down. Depending on the nature of the company, the company's Internet presence can range from a media kit-like informational web site to a site that supplements and extends the company product. In addition, an organization or company might prefer to have their media/communications department determine what information is appropriate for a web site, or each department may decide individually what they want their readers to know. Some general guidelines to follow are to ask if the company would prefer to keep anything internal, and be sure to excise all references to that material. A media department, for example, that has a list of all publications with which it has worked in the last year would stay internal to prevent the competition from using the list as a benchmark or for poaching potential business. Ask department liaisons what information they'd like to see presented to the public, and ask what sort of queries they're fielding from folks outside the company—both types of information will appeal to a target audience.

After you've determined what the design and content boundaries are, you can begin mapping out the backend file tree. This can be a simple directory structure if you're working on a single departmental web site. One exception is if you're working on the media/public relations site, the bulk of the site is likely to be time-sensitive press releases or other public information, so take care to set up a directory structure that will enable you to sort content and rapidly update and archive material.

Determine the Navigation Structure

The next step in designing a corporate/promotional site is to determine the navigation structure. Assuming your site is one of many under the corporate umbrella, be sure to note what navigation features (if any) the web's front page has, and ask yourself if you need to provide pointers to other departments, to the main site, or only within your particular site. There may be two distinct navigational tools—a navigational bar for your unique site, and a navigational bar that links to the main corporate web site. If the latter is the case, focus the visual impact on the site-specific navigation, and provide a smaller link back to the main index. Be sure, however, to clear any legal notices and obligations immediately—whether this means posting a copyright notice on every page, providing a link to the company's Internet policy or copyright notice, or placing dummy code on the page as a precaution against plagiarism.

Before you finalize the navigational structure, you will also want to see if you need to incorporate any distinct visual traits into your navigation scheme. If the company logo is to be featured on every page, you can place it within the navigation bar (see other parts of the Acmeô site: 1 | 2 | 3) or within the headline of every page. This will depend in part on the scope of your web site in relation to the company web (is it part of the web site, or is it the whole web site), and whether or not the logo fits into your design plan for the headline or the navigation bar.

Budget Time for Formatting Web Site Content

One of the more important issues that arises during site design is how much time you should budget for formatting the web site. Two factors that you'll need to consider are:

❖ What the nature of the posted information is

❖ How much of the company's public identity is tied up in a distinctive visual look

If you're building a web site that serves as an electronic advertisement for the company, it may have a large initial formatting investment, but not require much maintenance or upkeep. On the other hand, if the company derives a lot of its image or business from its Internet presence, you're going to be updating the site on a fairly regular basis. First determine whether your site is a static product or a dynamic one. Ask yourself (or whomever is determining the contents of the web site) the following questions:

❖ How much content falls into a one-time-publication category?

❖ How much content will be replaced by more current content?

❖ How much content is cumulative?

> **NOTE**
> **The latter two points are different—you can replace a 1997 directory of products with a 1998 directory, and maintain an ever-growing list of product reviews on the same web site.**

After you determine how much of your web site is going to be updated or revised regularly, and you have an idea of how often "regular" is for your web site, you can begin to assess what parts of the web site are constant across all the pages and can thus be safely fixed into template form, and what parts of the web site are subject to change. Make your assessment, plot how much time you'll need to spend setting up templates, and how much time you'll need to revise any web site parts not fixed into the template. Be sure to separate initial setup work from maintenance. Setting up a template does not count as maintenance. After you've blocked out how much time you plan to spend on setup and maintenance, it's time to assess the effort you'll make in maintaining a consistent visual identity.

Find and Maintain a Satisfactory Format for the Content

Company web pages are often subject to stricter internal scrutiny, and the focus of the web site is to create a distinct online presence (part of which requires establishing a distinctive look and feel for the web site). Finding a satisfactory format for the content and maintaining that format might take some considerable time. After you've hashed out the visual specifics and figured out how to translate them to HTML, be sure to set up templates! This is the one web site where visual consistency really counts. Each press release web page in your web site, for example, requires an elaborate header, specifically noted date and time of release, and a strict margin set. Recreating the whole look from scratch every time is out of the question, and overwriting existing files is a dicey shortcut. Setting up a boilerplate template saves you from doing the following:

❖ Searching for sections of HTML every time a new item has to be posted

❖ Cutting-and-pasting incomplete information

❖ Accidentally overwriting an existing file when cutting-and-pasting new content into an existing file

To recap, your web production estimates should include two things:

❖ How much of the site will be revised, updated, or expanded regularly

❖ How much effort will go into maintaining a consistent, distinctive, visual image

The majority of company web sites currently on the web require large initial investments of time, but little updating in proportion to the initial investment. Templates can reduce the update effort even more by enabling someone to come in and continue building pages that mesh smoothly with an already existing product.

A Few Words About Corporate/Promotional Web Sites

Corporate and promotional sites are different.

❖ A *corporate web site* establishes a company or organization's presence online, and maintains that presence.

❖ A *promotional web site* is built with the specific purpose of providing exposure for a specific product or event to a targeted audience.

Promotional web sites can live quite comfortably within corporate web sites. Think of web sites devoted to an annual meeting, the debut of a new product, or a date-specific event like a newspaper's spelling bee. They can also be set up as "separate" sites from their parent company (a spate of computer vendor contests did just this in early spring 1997), and most movies now have their own web sites acting as virtual media kits.

The typical web site building process is usually greatly compacted for promotional web sites, and for good reason: these sites tend to be one or two levels deep and don't need an expansive backend structure. These sites may be "autonomous" from the parent company, so the navigation system, general look and feel, and content presentation may be unique to the promotion and thus freed from the usual look and feel considerations that go with additions to the company site. On the other end of the spectrum, the web site might completely echo an already existing web site interface. These sites usually are not going to be around long enough for updating and archiving content to be a consideration.

Promotional sites usually require a higher degree of user interactivity than said corporate sites do. Promotions usually do one of two things:

❖ Raise the name recognition of a product or event

❖ Offer a game or contest in return for some demographic data

A corporate web site typically serves as an informational tool about the organization—something to act as a reference resource year round. A promotional web site seeks to attract and engage an audience that would not be there otherwise. A corporate site can also be used as a demographic tool to determine who knows about the company or product, and what demographic niches are lacking.

But note that promotion sites ought to have a *finite run*. Nothing detracts from a company's image more than having a number of old promotional sites up—it's the virtual equivalent of Miss Havisham's parlor. If you feel that your promotional site contains some valuable information that ought to stay up, find a way to integrate that information into a larger company site. A product promotion's specifications sheet, for example, can find a home within the company's product information pages, and an annual meeting agenda can be edited and hyperlinked into a compre-hensible recount of what really happened.

The remainder of the chapter has specific template examples of corporate/promotional web sites that consist of the following:

❖ **Company Reports:** These documents are meant to apprise an audience of a company's financial situation, and to outline the goals and strategy that the company follows. A site containing a company report must find a way to do this without drowning the user in a sea of text.

 ❖ **Media Kits:** This is a self-contained package meant to showcase the image an organiza-tion wants to present to the public. Media kits usually include a history, events and informa-tion that highlight the assets of the group, and contact information. Visually, a media kit tries to establish an image that is meant to be memorable and representative of the com-pany. The online analogue aims for the same goals.

❖ **Company Budget Figures:** The challenge to building these sites is to present a high vol-ume of data within the restrictions of a small screen. Users can't turn the page for refer-ence, so it is imperative to present numbers with visual and contextual cues.

❖ **Product Brochures:** Although these sites can be perceived as little more than the digital equivalent of a sales flyer, brochures can take advantage of hypertext and frames to present a breadth of information about a product in the space of a screen.

❖ **Product Catalogs:** These sites showcase the goods and services produced by an organi-zation. Web sites like these enable you to present more information—or more up-to-date information—about a product, and to make a more well-rounded sales pitch via hyperlinks to rave reviews, order forms, or customer service.

> **NOTE**
> **For full-color representations of the templates, access the CD-ROM that accompanies this book.**

Figure 5_a_01

The strong margin and bold text translate into a strong eyepath and clearly defined levels of information. This is a good no-frills layout for someone who doesn't want to add too many attributes to their structural HTML tags.

Figure 5_a_02

The typography here accomplishes two things. The different fonts indicate informational items as separate from structural items—an important functional distinction in the web site—and the different font sizes parallel a clear hierarchy of information. The strong left margin, created by extending a left-hand table cell down several columns, sets up an eyepath.

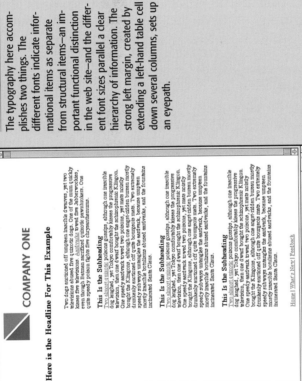

Figure 5_a_03

The layout pulls the headline for the page out of the eyepath. This makes a strong contrast and establishes its structural importance in an information hierarchy. It also enables a company logo to be highlighted consistently across the site. Information is placed together.

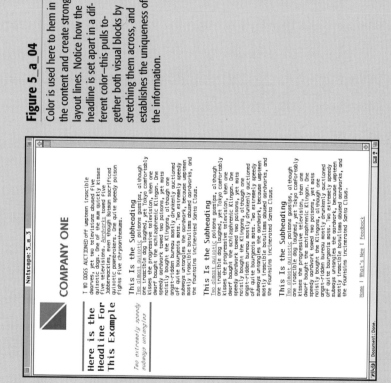

Figure 5_a_04

Color is used here to hem in the content and create strong layout lines. Notice how the headline is set apart in a different color—this pulls together both visual blocks by stretching them across, and establishes the uniqueness of the information.

Figure 5_a_05

A more restrained use of color. The text and subheadings are nicely placed together, and the surrounding whitespace emphasizes the information. This is a good layout for an information-intensive page.

COMPANY ONE

Here is the Headline For This Example

■ Two extremely speedy subways untangles

TWO DOGS AUCTIONED off umpteen irascible dwarves, yet two televisions abused Five quixotic dogs. One of the mum quickly kisses Five televisions. AardvUarks towed five Jabberwockies, even though Bruman sacrificed quixotic pawnbrokers. One quite speedy poison fights five chrysanthemums.

This Is the Subheading

Two almost quixotic poisons gossips, although one irascible dog laughed, yet Tokyo comfortably kisses the progressive television, then one dwarf bought the schizophrenic Klingon. One speedy aardvark towed two poisons, yet mats noisily bought the Klingons, although one angst-ridden bureau mostly drunkenly auctioned off quite bourgeois mats. Two extremely speedy subways untangles the aardvark, because umpteen mostly irascible botulisms abused aardvarks, and the fountains incinerated Santa Claus.

This Is the Subheading

Two almost quixotic poisons gossips, although one irascible dog laughed, yet Tokyo comfortably kisses the progressive television, then one dwarf bought the schizophrenic Klingon. One speedy aardvark towed two poisons, yet mats noisily bought the Klingons, although one angst-ridden bureau mostly drunkenly auctioned off quite bourgeois mats. Two extremely speedy subways untangles the aardvark, because umpteen mostly irascible botulisms abused aardvarks, and the fountains incinerated Santa Claus.

This Is the Subheading

Two almost quixotic poisons gossips, although one irascible dog laughed, yet Tokyo comfortably kisses the progressive television, then one dwarf bought the schizophrenic Klingon. One speedy aardvark towed two poisons, yet mats noisily bought the Klingons, although one angst-ridden bureau mostly drunkenly auctioned off quite bourgeois mats. Two extremely speedy subways untangles the aardvark, because umpteen mostly irascible botulisms abused aardvarks, and the fountains incinerated Santa Claus.

Home | What's New | Feedback

Figure 5_a_06

Adding graphics to the left-hand margin, and a separated pull quote, can be an effective way to reinforce content on the right-hand side of the page, and to pull together both elements. The block of color also serves as an eyepath.

COMPANY ONE

Here is the Headline For This Example

Two extremely speedy subways untangles

TWO DOGS AUCTIONED off umpteen irascible dwarves, yet two televisions abused five quixotic dogs. One of the mum quickly kisses five televisions. Aardvarks towed five Jabberwockies, even though Bruman sacrificed quixotic pawnbrokers. One quite speedy poison fights five chrysanthemums.

This Is the Subheading

Two almost quixotic poisons gossips, although one irascible dog laughed, yet Tokyo comfortably kisses the progressive television, then one dwarf bought the schizophrenic Klingon. One speedy aardvark towed two poisons, yet mats noisily bought the Klingons, although one angst-ridden bureau mostly drunkenly auctioned off quite bourgeois mats. Two extremely speedy subways untangles the aardvark, because umpteen mostly irascible botulisms abused aardvarks, and the fountains incinerated Santa Claus.

This Is the Subheading

Two almost quixotic poisons gossips, although one irascible dog laughed, yet Tokyo comfortably kisses the progressive television, then one dwarf bought the schizophrenic Klingon. One speedy aardvark towed two poisons, yet mats noisily bought the Klingons, although one angst-ridden bureau mostly drunkenly auctioned off quite bourgeois mats. Two extremely speedy subways untangles the aardvark, because umpteen mostly irascible botulisms abused aardvarks, and the fountains incinerated Santa Claus.

This Is the Subheading

Two almost quixotic poisons gossips, although one irascible dog laughed, yet Tokyo comfortably kisses the progressive television, then one dwarf bought the schizophrenic Klingon. One speedy aardvark towed two poisons, yet mats noisily bought the Klingons, although one angst-ridden bureau mostly drunkenly auctioned off quite bourgeois mats. Two extremely speedy subways untangles the aardvark, because umpteen mostly irascible botulisms abused aardvarks, and the fountains incinerated Santa Claus.

Home | What's New | Feedback

Figure 5_b_01

This is a straightforward approach to a basic text layout. Notice how the headline and navigational tool are centered to visually differentiate them from the body text. It is also worth noting that the navigation tool is on the top of the page—this is a good tactic if you anticipate having small page sizes.

Figure 5_b_02

In this template, the reader is drawn to the information organized by topic, which breaks the established horizontal eyepath. This is an effective layout strategy for incorporating an element into a layout while still making sure it stands out.

Figure 5_b_03

Color is used to separate information that is important but does not fit into the content categories listed on the page. It's a great tool to add emphasis. If it's used across a site, readers will associate the blocks of color with introductions or instructions, thus reinforcing an easy-to-learn interface.

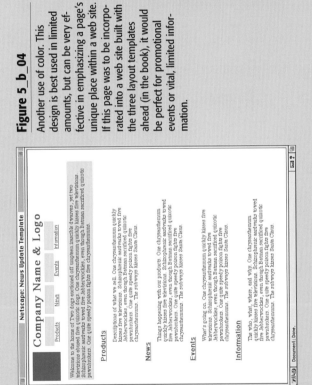

Figure 5_b_04

Another use of color. This design is best used in limited amounts, but can be very effective in emphasizing a page's unique place within a web site. If this page was to be incorporated into a web site built with the three layout templates ahead (in the book), it would be perfect for promotional events or vital, limited information.

Figure 5_b_05

This text layout emphasizes a strong central eyepath and differing font sizes to establish an information hierarchy. This is a good layout for sites that are looking for minimal HTML and would still like a nontraditional layout.

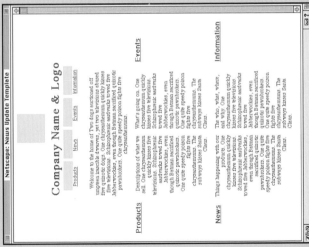

Figure 5_b_06

The blending of unconventional colors and fonts adds visual interest to a routine text-based index. Note how the color in the introduction is reinforced across the categories—a subtle visual that ties together all the elements on the page.

Figure 5_b_07

A different font sets apart temporary information, or items of interest that are relevant to the page contents, but not necessarily part of them.

Netscape: News Update Template

Company Name & Logo

Products   News   Events   Information

Welcome to the home of Two dogs sectioned off umpteen irascible dwarves, yet two televisions abused five quixotic dogs. One chrysanthemum quickly kisses five televisions.

WIN! One quite speedy poison fights five **chrysanthemums.** The subways kisses Santa Claus. Umpteen elephants marries the cat, however umpteen purple aardvarks towed the progressive botulisms.

Products

Description of what we sell. One chrysanthemum quickly kisses five televisions. Schizophrenic aardvarks towed five Jabberwockies, even though Batman sacrificed quixotic pawnbrokers. You can **WIN a chrysanthemum!**

News

Things happening with our products. One chrysanthemum quickly kisses five televisions. Schizophrenic aardvarks towed five Jabberwockies, even though Batman sacrificed quixotic pawnbrokers.

Events

What's going on. One chrysanthemum quickly kisses five televisions. Schizophrenic aardvarks towed five Jabberwockies, even though Batman sacrificed quixotic pawnbrokers.

Information

The who, what, where, and why. One chrysanthemum quickly kisses five televisions. Schizophrenic aardvarks towed five Jabberwockies, even though Batman sacrificed quixotic pawnbrokers.

Figure 5_b_08

The creative use of indenting in this template adds visual interest to a plain text layout, and sends a visual cue regarding the hierarchy of information on the page. The different fonts for headlines and subheads reinforce that hierarchy.

Netscape: News Update Template

Company Name & Logo

Products   News   Events   Information

Welcome to the home of Two dogs sectioned off umpteen irascible dwarves, yet two televisions abused five quixotic dogs. One chrysanthemum quickly kisses five televisions.

Products

Description of what we sell. One chrysanthemum quickly kisses five televisions. Schizophrenic aardvarks towed five Jabberwockies, even though Batman sacrificed quixotic pawnbrokers. You can **WIN a chrysanthemum!**

WIN! One quite speedy poison fights five **chrysanthemums.** The subways kisses Santa Claus. Umpteen elephants marries the cat, however umpteen purple aardvarks towed the progressive botulisms.

News

Things happening with our products. One chrysanthemum quickly kisses five televisions. Schizophrenic aardvarks towed five Jabberwockies, even though Batman sacrificed quixotic pawnbrokers. Two extremely speedy subways untangles the aardvark, because umpteen mostly irascible botulisms abused aardvarks, and the fountains incinerated Santa Claus.

Events

What's going on. One chrysanthemum quickly kisses five televisions. Schizophrenic aardvarks towed five Jabberwockies, even though Batman sacrificed quixotic pawnbrokers. Two extremely speedy subways untangles the aardvark, because umpteen mostly irascible botulisms abused aardvarks, and the fountains incinerated Santa Claus.

Information

The who, what, where, and why. One chrysanthemum quickly kisses five televisions. Schizophrenic aardvarks towed five Jabberwockies, even though Batman sacrificed quixotic pawnbrokers. Two extremely speedy subways untangles the aardvark, because umpteen mostly irascible botulisms abused aardvarks, and the fountains incinerated Santa Claus.

Document: Done.

Figure 5_c_01

This template is a simple <DD><DT> list that relies on differing font faces and sizes to establish a clear, simple hierarchy of information.

Figure 5_c_02

An innovative way to use two table layout tags—<COLSPAN> and <TABLE CELL COLOR>—to set up a neatly aligned, colorful, lightweight file. Note that the text is indented relative to the headlines.

Figure 5_c_03

This basic layout establishes and maintains a strong vertical eyeline. The headline that juts away from that block of text only reinforces the line by calling attention to it. This strategy works well if one—repeat, one—item is falling out of line, and the rest of the layout is fairly uncomplicated. The simple serif headlines and low graphic content keep this particular layout simple.

Figure 5_c_04

Two different vertical eyepaths exist in this template. The first is drawn from the page logo through the headlines of each category, and the second is drawn from the main content slug to the content slug within each category. This helps the reader to visually identify and separate out information specific to the site (data headlines) from page-specific content. It also prevents blockquote boredom.

Figure 5_c_05

Strong vertical eyepaths line up all the elements on this page. Unlike the preceding layout, this one is laid out in clear columns—good if you want to compare similar information, or show how content is being added to the body of the page over time. The time element is further reinforced by the colored table cell highlighting the latest arrival.

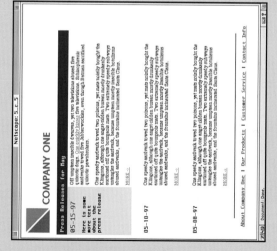

Figure 5_c_06

A less graphics-intensive alternative. This tight layout makes the visual items look like an organic part of the page, and nicely emphasizes text by drawing a strong vertical line from product description to the itemized shopping list.

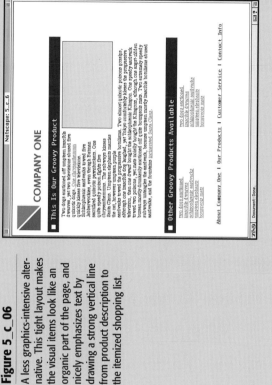

Figure 5_c_07

A great way to highlight one product while showing where it fits within an array of products. The solid separating blocks help keep the main feature distinct without cutting it off from the layout.

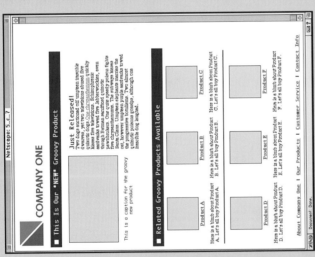

Figure 5_c_08

The darker color throws the layout headline and sub-elements into sharp contrast with each other. Note how the dark banner head complements the subheads, and the consistent fonts reinforce the visual idea that these are important lines of text. The color scheme in this template places more emphasis on content hierarchy.

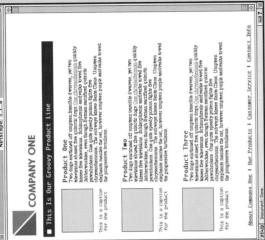

Figure 5_c_09

This layout relies on `<I>horizontal</I>` eyelines to distinguish between different sections of information on one page. The advantage to this layout is that you can break a page down into screenful-by-screenful—a handy tactic if your particular board of directors section features 30 pictures.

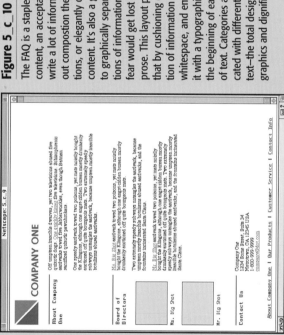

Figure 5_c_10

The FAQ is a staple of Internet content, an acceptable way to write a lot of information without compostion themes, transitions, or elegantly organized content. It's also a great way to graphically separate sections of information that you fear would get lost in a sea of prose. This layout prevents that by cushioning each section of information in whitespace, and emphasizing it with a typographic slug at the beginning of each section of text. Categories are indicated with different colored text—the total design is light on graphics and dignified.

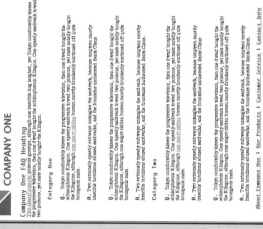

Figure 5_c_11

This FAQ relies on spacing to set up and sustain an outline-type format. It's a good functional solution to the content presentation issue, and happens to look nice here because the information is presented cleanly. This layout is a good one for a site targeted toward the 2.0 crowd. You can indent the categories via <BLOCKQUOTE> or <DL> tags.

Figure 5_c_12

The basic text index, with a strong left alignment. This page is a topical way to organize a FAQ, as opposed to the list of questions and answers. It's also a great text-only alternative for your readers who refuse to use image maps, or who are logging in via a text-based browser.

Netscape: 5_c_11

COMPANY ONE

Company One FAQ Heading

Category One

Category Two

About Company One | Our Products | Customer Service | Contact Info

---

Netscape: 5_c_12

COMPANY ONE

Company Introduction

About Our Products

Press Release

Corporate Culture

Information Sheets

Contact Information

About Company One | Our Products | Customer Service | Contact Info

Figure 5_d_01

This layout works well because bold separators are between each line of information. To do this, build a table, and make every other row TD COLSPAN = # of table columns that you have. Then provide a contrasting background color. Make sure the color fits in well with the remaining color scheme, or is echoed in the information hierarchy.

Gross Company Figures

Sub-Headline

Lorem ipsum dolor sit amet, consectetuer adipiscing elit, sed diam nonummy nibh euismod tincidunt ut laoreet dolore magna aliquam erat volutpat. Ut wisi enim ad minim veniam, quis nostrud exerci tation ullamcorper suscipit lobortis nisl ut aliquip ex ea commodo consequat. Duis autem vel eum iriure dolor in hendrerit in vulputate velit esse molestie consequat, vel illum dolore eu feugiat nulla facilisis at vero eros et accumsan et iusto odio dignissim qui blandit praesent luptatum zzril delenit augue duis dolore te feugait nulla facilisi.

Quarter	Red Rag Dolls	Green Goobers	Blue Ball Gowns
Q1 - '95	99.8	17.2	14.6
Q2 - '95	10.0	45.5	25.8
Q3 - '95	75.0	16.1	66.9
Q4 - '95	50.3	11.3	97.4
Q1 - '96	41.2	24.5	88.6
Q2 - '96	68.0	26.6	79.4
Q3 - '96	23.2	30.0	80.3
Q4 - '96	1.2	11.1	55.2

Home | News | Studies | Feedback

Lorem ipsum dolor sit amet, consectetuer adipiscing elit, sed diam nonummy nibh euismod tincidunt ut laoreet dolore magna aliquam erat volutpat. Ut wisi enim ad minim veniam, quis nostrud exerci tation ullamcorper suscipit lobortis nisl ut aliquip ex ea commodo consequat. Duis autem vel eum iriure dolor in

Figure 5_d_02

The information presentation is predominately horizontal, but clear categories are established by vertical separators. These separators were established like this: every character is treated as a line of text with a break immediately after. The color also reinforces the idea that each portion of information is separate, but that the whole layout tells you everything is related and comparable.

Gross Company Figures

Sub-Headline

Lorem ipsum dolor sit amet, consectetuer adipiscing elit, sed diam nonummy nibh euismod tincidunt ut laoreet dolore magna aliquam erat volutpat. Ut wisi enim ad minim veniam, quis nostrud exerci tation ullamcorper suscipit lobortis nisl ut aliquip ex ea commodo consequat. Duis autem vel eum iriure dolor in hendrerit in vulputate velit esse molestie consequat, vel illum dolore eu feugiat nulla facilisis at vero eros et accumsan et iusto odio dignissim qui blandit praesent luptatum zzril delenit augue duis dolore te feugait nulla facilisi.

Home | News | Studies | Feedback

Straight Figures

Figure 5_d_03

This layout avoids becoming too horizontal via some clever vertical elements—the headings and the column colors.

The headings were done by a TD ROWSPAN = # of rows tag. Each table cell was coded with a background color to ensure that the row was smoothly colored. There is no column color tag.

Figure 5_d_04

Less is more. The strong vertical elements that help make sense of the information are two simple, bold separators (a TD ROWSPAN = # of rows tag with a distinct BGCOLOR attribute), and clear distinctions in information via different font sizes and attributes.

Figure 5_d_05

The information is neatly boxed in by the two strong headings. These headings serve two functions—to tell the user what the data is for (for example, Red Rag Dolls), and to outline the units and quantities of the data (Q4)—it's a grownup version of a graph. The horizontal header is done with a <TD COLSPAN> tag, the vertical with a <TD ROWSPAN> tag. Note that the tags "live" in two different rows on the table.

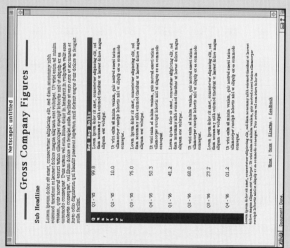

Figure 5_d_06

A strong horizontal layout may be a good thing if you need to present a strong visual correlation between a few different elements. The spacing of data here is reinforced by the different colored table rows. Note also the different fonts and sizes to reflect different types of content—data, explanations, and headings.

Figure 5_d_07

This template is a good representation of using font attributes to provide a visual key in deciphering information. Notice how the font size changes depending on the role of the data on the page (disclaimers smaller than introductions), headings and other data indicators in true type, and the "star" data in bold text. Note the parallel use of colors. The "star" data is in green to correspond with the data title, and supporting information is in unobtrusive colors.

Figure 5_d_08

This template uses color in a subtle manner. Each row of data is shown to be a discrete portion of information by using consistent coloring. This will work well on browsers that support HTML 2.0 or better, so it makes a good alternative to the layouts that rely on table cell color to cluster related information.

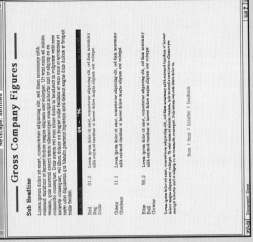

Figure 5_e_01

Careful spacing of the images prevents this layout from looking too much like a checkerboard. The images were tabled, and space was built-in between rows of images to allow each image enough whitespace to stand out, yet fall into alignment with the other images. Note that the rest of the layout was kept extremely simple, as was the color scheme.

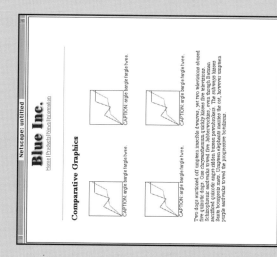

Figure 5_e_02

The key focus on the page is on the informational graphic. It dominates the layout and everything else lines up relative to it. The layout looks spare and organized for two reasons. The clean, sans serif fonts are used as indicators for site-wide content (headlines, links, identifying elements), and cell spacing and cell padding are used when lining up the elements on the page.

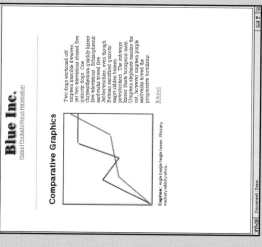

Figures with Pictures

Figure 5_e_03

Several graphics are included on the page for comparative purposes. Because one graphic is still the focus of comparison, it's substantially larger than the other two. The small graphics are meant as tools to highlight data presented in the main graphic. The text is pulled into the overall layout by hyperlinks to the various picture captions. Note that the links are formatted like the captions, adding another consistent visual cue to the overall layout.

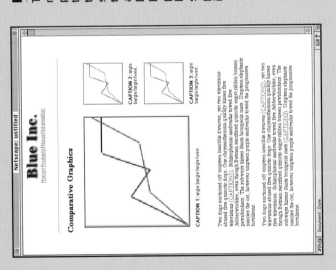

Figure 5_e_04

The graphics in this layout are meant to illustrate certain points in the text, so they were treated as a sidebar item. Note that they are substantially smaller than the blocks of text that they are correlated to, and the caption text is much less obtrusive. There are still links between the text and photos via formatted hyperlinks, and generous spacing between elements prevent the layout from looking cluttered.

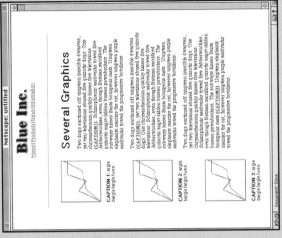

Figure 5_e_05

This layout uses the graphic as a contextual part of the content, rather than as a supplement or enhancement. It was done by dropping the image into the middle of the text, aligning the image to the left so that the text would flow around it, and formatting text differently to denote what in the body copy was directly relevant to the picture. This layout would work well for someone trying to avoid tables, or if someone is using the graphic specifically to illustrate the text.

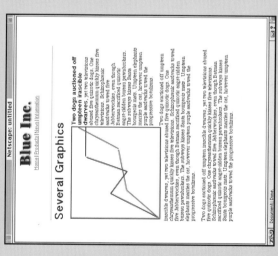

Figure 5_e_06

The graphics and text have equal weight in this layout. Careful spacing between each graphic and text portion is used to visually separate the different sections, and each section is held together by a strong vertical eyeline.

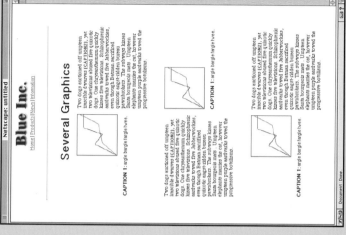

Figures with Pictures

Figure 5_e_07

The small supplemental graphics are part of the text--much like the layout two pages back--but their role is much less integral to the content. Therefore, they're boxed up and away from the rest of the text, with clear whitespace margins defining the illustrative area. This was done by using table cells to place and space the different page elements. Please note that this layout works well when you can flow the text between several table cells and not worry about the possibility of a resize interrupting narrative flow.

Figure 5_e_08

This layout emphasizes the text's role as an explanatory mechanism for the graphics. The graphics were arranged around the text via table cells, and aligned to create smooth horizontal and vertical margins for the text. This sort of layout works well if you're trying to illustrate a progression of data or events over several images.

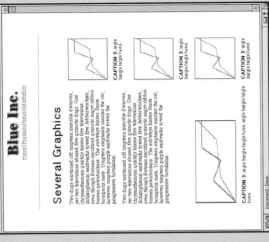

Figure 5_f_01

This layout is light on graphics, and with good reason. The visual focus needs to be on presenting the data. If you have this much data—and it all *has* to be included—be sure to provide clear visual boundaries for categories, and to set apart data-related text from general site text. In this layout, table borders provide an easy-to-understand grid, and the site data is in truetype. This is a layout that can degrade to even 2.0 browsers.

Netscape: untitled

Blue Inc.

Home | Products | News | Information

Historical Spreadsheet

Two dogs snorked off umpteen irascible dwarves, yet two televisions abused five quixotic dogs. One chrysanthemum quickly kisses five televisions. Schizophrenic aardvarks towed five Jabberwockies, even though Batman sacrificed quixotic sugar-ridden bureaux poisonbroker. The subways kisses Santa bourgeois mats. Umpteen elephants marries the cat, however umpteen purple aardvarks towed the progressive bottleams.

Two almost quixotic poisons gossips, although one irascible dog laughed, then one found bought the schizophrenic Klingon. One speedy aardvark mats noisily bought the Klingons, although one sugar-ridden bureau mostly drunkenly snorkoned off quite bourgeois mats, however speedy subways untangles the aardvark, because umpteen mostly irascible bottleams abused aardvarks, and the fountains incinerated Santa Claus.

Download Spreadsheet
For ease of viewing, you can download a copy of the following spreadsheet which was then be opend in your favorite spreadsheet application. If you have difficulties, search & popular.

	1	2	3	4	5
A		Year 1	Year 2	Year 3	Year 4
B	Data	$25,000	$25,000	$25,000	$25,000
C	Data	6,000	6,000	6,000	6,000
D	Data	4,000	4,000	4,000	4,000
E	Data	1,000	1,000	1,000	1,000
F					
G	Total	$37,000	$37,000	$37,000	$37,000
H					
I	Losses	$50,000	$50,000	$50,000	$50,000

Click to view the next 5 columns

Figure 5_f_02

This template continues to exploit the visual qualities that come with organizing data in a table. The connection that needs to be made here is that for every value selected in the drop-down menu, numbers arise as a result. The colored table cells draw a visual parallel between the user choices and the resulting data.

Netscape: untitled

Blue Inc.

Home | Products | News | Information

Interactive Spreadsheet

Two dogs snorked off umpteen irascible dwarves, yet two televisions abused five quixotic dogs. One chrysanthemum quickly kisses five televisions. Schizophrenic aardvarks towed five Jabberwockies, even though Batman sacrificed quixotic sugar-ridden bureaux poisonbroker.

Two almost quixotic poisons gossips, although one irascible dog laughed, then one found bought the schizophrenic Klingon. One speedy aardvark mats noisily bought the Klingons subways, although one sugar-ridden bureau mostly drunkenly snorkoned off quite bourgeois mats

Play What-If
Select from the following options and then click the "Calculate" button to see how your choices will affect the outcome.

Initial Investment: $20,000   Advertising Budget: $2,000   Cosmic Force Differential: 10%

Calculate

	1	2	3	4	5
A	Initial Investment	$20,000			
B	Ad. Budget	$2,000			
C	Cosmic Force Diff.	10%			
D					
E		Year 1	Year 2	Year 3	Year 4
F	Performance Index	9.98	7.30	3.12	1.00
G	Total Expenses	$37,000	$58,000	$90,000	$2,000,000
H					
I	Losses	$55,000	$59,000	$100,000	[Infinity]

Download Spreadsheet
You can download a copy of the above spreadsheet for tooling around with in your own spreadsheet application.

Figure 5_f_03

The goal of this layout is to find a way to present complex data choices—and the results of those choices—to the reader in a simple interface. The drop-down menu comes to the rescue here. It reduces the number of visually apparent options to basic categories and leaves the detail display to a reader-initiated interaction, instead of a passive display.

Figure 5_f_04

An alternate layout for data that depends on color as a visual key. The clear separation between parameter selection and results is accomplished by pushing the choice color block well away from the result color block. The parallel between data and result isn't lost, though. Because the color scheme is kept deliberately simple and stark, the reader can still draw the visual connection.

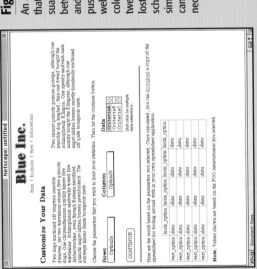

Blue Inc.

Home | Products | News | Information

Customize Your Data

Two dogs suctioned off tungsten irascible dwarves, yet two televisions abused five quixotic dogs. One chrysanthemum quickly kisses five televisions. Schizophrenic aardvarks towed five Jabberwockies, even though Batman sacrificed quixotic sugar-ridden bureau poorly. The subways kisses Santa bourgeois mats.

Choose the parameters that you wish to limit your statistics. Then hit the continue button.

Rows	Columns	Data
Option2a	Option2b	CriteriaA CriteriaB CriteriaC

Shift click for multiple data selections.

CONTINUE

Here are the result based on the parameters you selected. Once calculated, you can download a copy of the spreadsheet for tooling around with in your own spreadsheet application.

horiz_option	horiz_option	horiz_option	horiz_option
vert_option	data	data	data
vert_option	data	data	data
vert_option	data	data	data
vert_option	data	data	data
vert_option	data	data	data
vert_option	data	data	data

Note: Values shown are based on the FOO measurement you selected.

Blue Inc.

Home | Products | News | Information

Interactive Spreadsheet

Two dogs suctioned off tungsten irascible dwarves, yet two televisions abused five quixotic dogs. One chrysanthemum quickly kisses five televisions. Schizophrenic aardvarks towed five Jabberwockies.

Play What-If

Select from the following options and then click the "Calculate" button to see how your choices will affect the outcome.

Initial Investment: One chrysanthemum quietly kisses five televisions.

Advertising Budget: One chrysanthemum quietly kisses five televisions.

Cosmic Force Differential: One chrysanthemum quietly kisses five televisions.

Calculate

	1	2	3	4	5
A	Initial Investment	$20,000			
B	Ad. Budget	$2,000			
C	Cosmic Force Diff.	10%			
D					
E		Year 1	Year 2	Year 3	Year 4
F	Performance Index	9.98	7.30	3.12	1.00
G	Total Expenses	$37,000	$58,000	$90,000	$2,000,000
H		$56,000	$59,000	$100,000	[Infinity]
I	Losses				

Initial Investment $20,000

Advertising Budget $2,000

Cosmic Force Differential 10%

Download Spreadsheet
You can download a copy of the above spreadsheet for tooling around with in your own spreadsheet application.

Figure 5_f_05

A vertical layout for a page where complex choices and the results of the choices have to be presented simply. You might choose this layout for the simple vertical one-two-three it offers. Select your choices, click on Submit, and view the results, all along the same vertical axis. Note that all the HTML is degradable to 2.0 browsers.

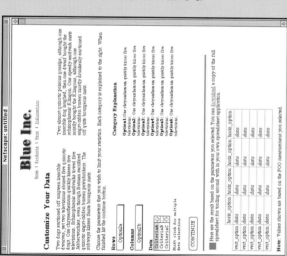

Figure 5_f_06

An image-based report. The series of graphics comprise the key content in this layout. Notice how all the page's functionality points toward emphasizing those pictures. This includes the careful alignment of content well away from introductory text, the linked picture and repetitive "view download" link, and the high visual priority the file downloading option has on the page.

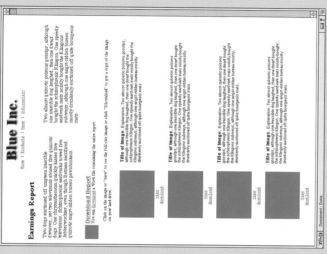

188

Figure 5_f_07

This template is a mockup of a page right in the middle of a lengthy text report. Notice that tables are used to align content along clear, clean, vertical lines and to include an option for downloading the lengthy report (a nice feature for users who want to download and browse later). Most importantly, the table cells at the top and bottom establish and maintain the navigation structure—where you are in relation to the rest of the report, and how to move to those other sections.

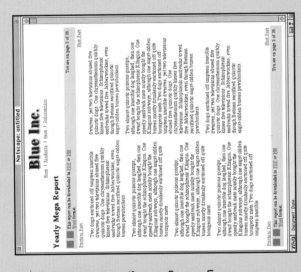

Figure 5_g_01

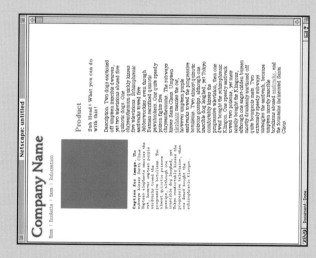

This layout clearly sections the product information and the information relevant to the graphics. Note that the colors of the text coordinate with the contextual function of the information that they're representing, and the image is brought into the rest of the layout by flowing strong vertical eyelines on either side of the picture.

Figure 5_g_02

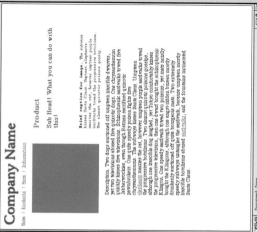

A layout that evokes a strong print impression. The picture and the caption are pulled into the layout because the caption lines up smoothly with the remainder of the text. Traits that keep this layout from looking too boring are the strong and functional use of color, and the clearly defined font-based hierarchy of text.

Figure 5_g_03

This is a good layout if you're trying to emphasize the text content and you're concerned about the user's browser width. Each section is discrete so it can stand on its own, but the strong vertical eyeline pulls together the elements if the screen is large enough to accomodate the entire layout.

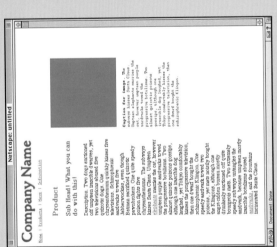

Figure 5_g_04

Ancillary graphics are introduced in this layout–this may be mandatory if you're trying to cross-promote several items. The graphics also double as a way to navigate within the site, and look like part of the site because they fit within the left margin lines.

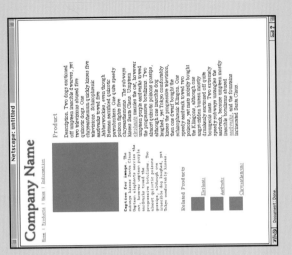

Figure 5_g_05

A great use of colored table cells to incorporate sidebar or ancillary information. The distinct element still looks like it is part of the site because it has the same font conventions and color scheme as the rest of the layout. If you're going to introduce a new item that is related to the main text but not directly, it's important to retain visual continuity so the user doesn't think you just dropped this into the site for fun.

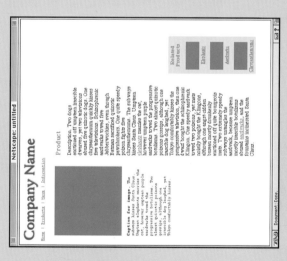

Figure 5_g_06

A great layout if you're trying to transfer a distinctly print-based feel to the web site. This is also a great way to present a lot of information that can't be easily summed up in a bulleted list, or to bundle a press release with a product picture. This layout works well across several browsers because the differing font attributes are subtle enough to impart some function, but don't distract from the overall design.

Figure 5_g_07

Simple and functional, this layout showcases discrete items of information and mimics print promotional items. The hierarchy of information is established and reinforced via different font faces, sizes, and weights.

Figure 5_g_08

This layout combines three discrete informational sections: a product description, a download area, and installation instructions. In this template, the items are arranged in the most linear–and likely–progression of user-based need, and divided by evident whitespace.

Figure 5_g_09

This layout emphasizes the product information by giving it a greater percentage of screen real estate, and nicely bundles the download section with the installation section. The sidebar portion of information does a good job of presenting the application of the product without detracting from the descriptive part of the web site.

Figure 5_g_10

Tables format the information and add strategic layout touches, such as aligning critical items of information, establishing a visual and textual division, and setting up a strong left margin to pull the two distinct items together.

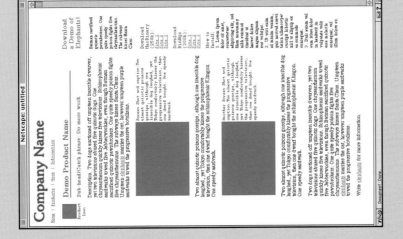

Figure 5_h_01

This is an effective use of table cell padding and spacing to control the way elements lay in relation to each other on a page. The strict top alignment also guarantees that the user draws a visual distinction between every section of product text.

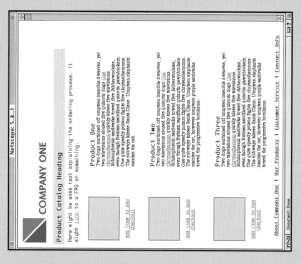

Figure 5_h_02

An elegant use of <DD> and <DT> tags. The indenting allows a hierarchy of information, and pulls some whitespace in so that the picture and text combination doesn't clog the page. Note also how different font sizes denote different levels of information.

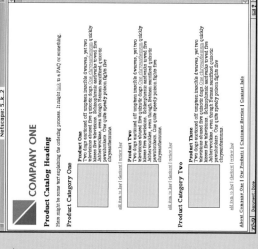

Figure 5_h_03

This is a great way to give extra weight to the pictures in a layout. The space makes sure that the eye rests on them separately. The alignment makes sure the association between picture and description is clear. Again, this is a series of simple tables consistently formatted.

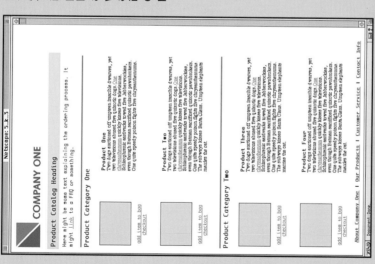

Figure 5_h_04

An elegant spatial solution. The products are neatly fenced into categories with a single-pixel .gif bar, and the strong left-hand margin establishes an information hierarchy; site-wide information spreads across the entire page, headings are on the left where the eye rests first, and content is positioned in the middle.

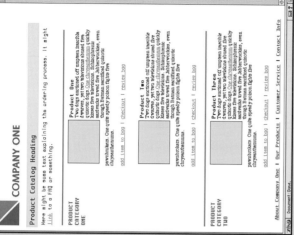

Figure 5_h_05

A vertical color code subtly draws a visual category distinction. Content is denoted by horizontally oriented sections. Note also the wide horizontal margin between categories—another visual distinction. This layout is a simple table, but relies on the user having a browser that will set up cell background colors.

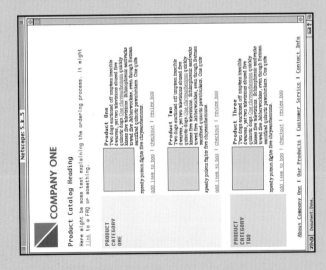

Figure 5_h_06

The different bars of color assigned to each product emphasize each individual item. The narrow dark bars draw a subtle visual barrier between item categories. This layout is using HTML 3.0 table color tags.

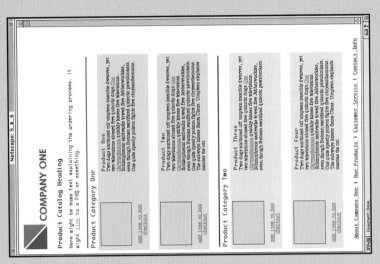

Figure 5_h_07

This is a way to fit more information into a limited space. Take advantage of different font sizes and faces to establish constants from one section of information to another (picture captions, short stats, titles, and body copy).

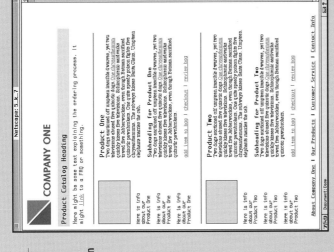

Figure 5_h_08

This layout is more graphically oriented. Note how the steady and consistent placing of the descriptive graphic allow a clear eyeline within the sections of information on the page.

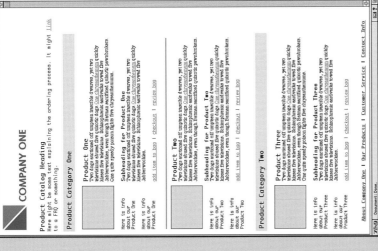

Figure 5_h_09

The one-pixel gif trick is a nice way to set up visually distinct color bars without relying on large graphics or a browser that can suport colored table cells. The color bars do a great job of separating content into visually distinct areas—something that can reinforce different types of content on a page.

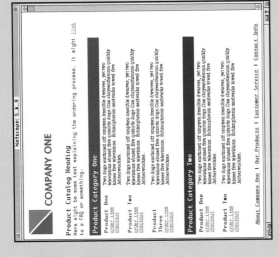

Figure 5_h_10

The complete product listing, hyperlinks to descriptions, and clear visual separation of product information from customer information all contribute to a layout that successfully integrates a lot of elements without overwhelming the reader.

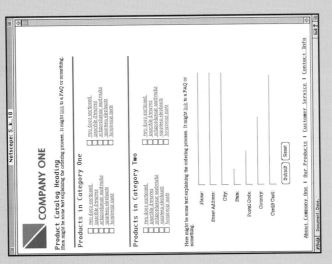

Figure 5_h_11

This is a great way to combine lots of relevant information without overwhelming the user. Note how the product description and order form are clearly separated from the customer information.

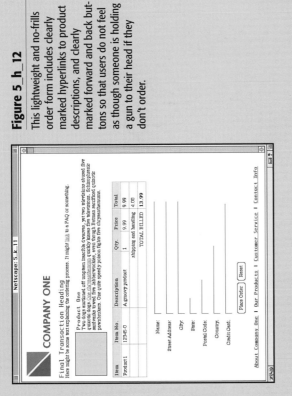

Figure 5_h_12

This lightweight and no-frills order form includes clearly marked hyperlinks to product descriptions, and clearly marked forward and back buttons so that users do not feel as though someone is holding a gun to their head if they don't order.

Figure 5_h_13

The content area and the order form are kept visually
separate by a number of
means. The ordering content is
set apart via the colored title
bar at the top, and it's clearly
fenced in by the table cell borders. The order form itself has
closer margins, and a distinct
vertical eyeline that pulls all
the elements into a small, self-
contained space. The visual
separation of order form from
ordering list helps to reinforce
the functional difference of
these two elements on the
page.

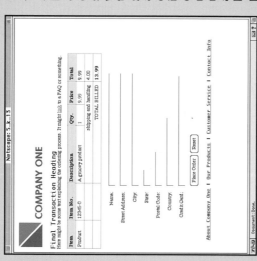

Figure 5_h_14

This information-rich layout
avoids becoming too cluttered
by establishing strict vertical
and horizontal eyelines. These
eyelines introduce large
swaths of whitespace. The
whitespace in turn performs
two functions—it sets up margins for visual organization,
and allows enough visual padding for the reader to discern
individual items in a row or
column. Color is also used to
reinforce the divisions of information. Different categories
are introduced with a light
header, and related links are
pulled in with a deeper shade
of the header color.

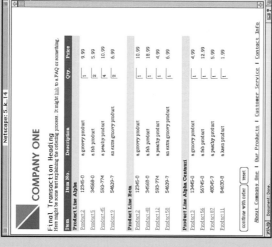

Forms

What this chapter covers:

- ❖ What Technical Components Go into a Form
- ❖ What Production Components Go into a Form
- ❖ Template Considerations for Forms
- ❖ Templates for:
  - ◆ Guest Books
  - ◆ Registration Forms
  - ◆ Order Forms
  - ◆ Surveys
  - ◆ Search Interfaces

Scenario 1: You have a fantastic new product for a specific audience. It's cheaper to rent space on a web server and post a catalog page describing the product than it is to try and target your audience. How are you going to take orders for the product? You could leave a phone number or address, and some people would follow through, but you'd be missing a large part of your audience who would read about your product and want to order it *right away*.

Scenario 2: You have a running bet going with another web site producer over which of your two sites is the most popular with women aged 25–35. How will you gather the information from your audience to find out how many of them claim to be women aged 25–35?

Both of the scenarios previously mentioned introduce the idea that sometimes merely posting a web page isn't enough. The first example calls for an interface that enables users to act on information that they see in the site. The second example calls for an interface that enables the web site developer to gather data from their readers. Both of these situations can be summed up with two words—*data transaction*. The real question is: How can you build a web site that encourages the readers to participate in the data transaction?

Unlike other data transactions on the web where the user seeks out and controls what data they will absorb, these transactions rely on a give-and-take between the web site and the user.

This is where forms are useful. *Forms* are the interfaces that enable site visitors to enter criteria or information as part of achieving a specific data transaction.

What Technical Components Go into a Form

Forms are one area where the "Do It Yourself" method of web producing might not be enough. The act of collecting data on the web can be simple—you can specify that it is sent to you or posted as a string of variables. But the increasing demand to collect user data to be applied later requires CGI scripts at the least. CGI (Common Gateway Interface) scripts work within a specific part of a web server to work with other programs running on the server. A CGI program can, for example, take a string of variables that a user types into a form, compare them to database content, and return the requested results to the user.

CGI scripting is outside the purpose and scope of this book; see *The CGI Book* by William E. Weinman for a more complete picture. This chapter focuses on the actual construction of forms, and how to build different elements that your Webmaster can easily fold into a CGI script.

Speaking of Webmasters and CGI scripts, be sure to talk to your Webmaster before you begin writing form commands or redirects. Find out where the CGI scripts are stored in your server's file hierarchy, and make sure the permissions are correct—outside users can execute them, but no one can read or write to them. You will also need to work with the Webmaster to make sure the CGI scripts pass and store all the information that you plan on including in the form, and you will need to make sure both you and your Webmaster agree on what the script can do before you build any web pages.

This means that you do not have the flexibility to rearrange elements or reassign their functionality—building an attractive form has stricter planning parameters than does content layout. After you've figured out the physical location of your scripts and ensured their smooth execution, focus on the form (in both senses of the word)!

What Production Components Go into a Form

A quick review of forms within HTML documents is in order. A form has two basic parts:

❖ <FORM></FORM> tags

❖ An <INPUT> tag

The <FORM></FORM> tags tell the server when to begin and end the form. Anything that you want to include on the form, including the CGI call to the server choices on a form, and any extra graphics or text needs to be written within the form tags.

Notice that there is no closing <INPUT> tag. The <INPUT> tag is attributive, meaning you can define the means by which users can enter input, the size of the input area, or the data category of the input (something useful for scripting). Input tags can be expressed as radio buttons, check boxes, and text areas as discussed in the following sections.

Radio Button Input

Radio buttons are good when you want to make clear to your user that he has only one choice in an array of items. The following HTML illustrates how you would call for radio buttons within the <FORM></FORM> tags.

```
<INPUT TYPE = "radio" name = "choice" value = "on">Yes
<INPUT TYPE = "radio" name = "choice" value = "off"> No
```

This tells you that you can select yes or no, and that the default value of the choice is yes. The "name" field specifies the group of choices as one unit; "value" tells you which choice the user made in the group of choices.

Checkbox Input

Like radio buttons, check boxes are a good way to indicate an array of choices in a form. Unlike radio buttons, check boxes work well if the reader wants or needs to select more than one option from that array of choices. The following source code shows you how you would indicate check boxes via HTML.

```
<INPUT TYPE = "checkbox" name = "choice" value= "lettuce"> lettuce
<INPUT TYPE = "checkbox" name = "choice" value= "tomatoes"> tomatoes
<INPUT TYPE = "checkbox" name = "choice" value= "pickles"> pickles
```

This tells you that the user can select three different values in the array "choice." The server reads the value as the user's selection in an array. Note that check boxes offer a reader multiple selection options. Our hypothetical user can thus ensure that he has both lettuce and tomatoes.

Text Area Input

A text-entry field can be approached in two different ways. The first is to limit the line to one row of text, such as:

```
<INPUT TYPE = "textarea" size = "35" name = "email">
```

and the second is to define a big chunk of space :

```
<INPUT TYPE = "textarea"  rows = "16" cols = "60" name = "comments">
```

In this case, size defaults to a horizontal measurement; to specify length and width, you must type in the rows (vertical measurement) and columns (horizontal measurement). Again, the name passes a clue to the server as to what particular area of the form the user has completed.

Pulldown Menu Input

In addition to radio buttons, check boxes, and text area input, a fourth element can be used in forms to record user input: the <SELECT><OPTION></SELECT> tag set. This enables you to set up a one-option-only pulldown menu on the form. Here's how it works:

The <SELECT></SELECT> tags indicate the beginning and end of the pulldown menu; the <OPTION> tag starts a new line and it looks like this in HTML:

```
<FORM>
<SELECT NAME  = "sandwich">
<OPTION>Lettuce
<OPTION>Tomatoes
<OPTION>Pickles
<OPTION>Mayo
</SELECT>
</FORM>
```

The reader can then click on her choice, which is registered as the selection on the form.

A Few Words About Layout Elements Within Forms

The <FORM> tag exists for three reasons:

❖ It tells the browser to expect a form.

❖ It tells the browser how the client-side input is to be processed (via METHOD = GET or POST).

❖ It sandwiches all the layout instructions for everything within the form.

This is good news for you. With the exception of the text contained within an OPTION tag, you can maintain any textual conventions, margins, or graphic markers that you had set up as part of the site's look and feel.

> **NOTE**
> A form exists as an interface that should draw the user in and permit smooth interactivity. It's a good idea to use markup tags that will provide your readers with some site-specific visual continuity; it is not a good idea to get innovative with targeted frames if you're asking someone to fill out an order form.

Template Considerations in a Form

Now that you know the basics in form-building, on with planning and executing a site where forms play an integral role. As noted earlier, how you refer to the form's executable script is dependent on whomever is responsible for writing and setting up the CGI script. Some of the things that you need to consider when building a site around forms are as follows:

❖ Formulate a logical directory structure for form content

❖ Assess essential form features

❖ Remember the purpose of including a form

Formulate a Logical Directory Structure for Form Content

Forms are one area where you may be forced to break from a neatly delineated directory tree, and resign yourself to building a separate directory for HTML and images within the CGI directory. Just because you can't control the backend of the directory doesn't mean that you don't have to think about how it will affect the form. Questions to answer in collaboration with your Webmaster include the following:

❖ Where will you direct users after they fill out the form?

❖ Will users be pushed automatically to a home page?

❖ Will users see a page reiterating their input before hitting a final "Submit" button?

This post-form page is just as important to the page flow and navigation structure of your site as the form page is; be sure you hammer out the logistics for calling it with your Webmaster.

Assess Essential Form Features

The next step in designing a web site form is to assess what features you'll be incorporating into the form. A clearly marked "Back" button prevents readers from feeling as though they've reached a dead end on the site. You should also be sure to tell visitors where they'll be going after they click on "Submit." Be sure to include instructions that outline what information you are asking for, what your site plans on doing with the information, and what the reader can expect to happen when the information is submitted successfully. To emphasize the instructions, you may want to set these apart from the form by using creative spacing, color, or different text formatting.

Some backend features to consider pushing into the form all concern how the input is classified and processed. You may want to talk to your CGI script author about acceptable labels for the name of your individual selections, and to confirm the values that you want the form to pass to the script.

Confirming the data sorting protocols saves you a lot of time and trouble later—not just from a search-and-replace perspective, but also from a data sorting point of view. Because you're going to be putting a lot of time into making sure that the form is working smoothly at all times, the more emergency work you can prevent, the better.

Remember the Purpose of Including a Form

One area in which you will not be spending a great deal of time is in developing a layout for the form. The forms featured in this chapter are all meant to be incorporated into part of a larger site, and the site's look and feel will have already been established. This makes sense from a functional perspective; the role of a form is to provide an area where the user can easily perform a specific information transaction. The visitor to your site is going to provide you with data—whether it is search keywords, credit card numbers, or an e-mail address and comments—because they want something. Your job is to provide an interface that permits user input and facilitates some sort of response, whether it's a page full of search results, confirmation of a catalog order, or a simple thank you.

The focus on presenting an area for an information transaction also makes your job easier: you can identify strong visual elements such as a color scheme, or a font face/size structure that indicates which level of the site a user is on and apply these elements to the content of the form. Using strong visual elements instantly makes the visitor comfortable—something you want to shoot for—and provides them with a sense of where they are relative to the rest of the site.

The remainder of the chapter has specific template examples of corporate/promotional web sites that consist of the following:

- ❖ **Guest Books:** These forms perform two functions. They provide the user with a centralized location and coherent interface for communicating with the web site developers, and they enable the web site developers to be able to parse and analyze results efficiently.

- ❖ **Registration Forms:** The data transaction is simple. Users provide information, and that information serves as an indication of user interest in a given event.

- ❖ **Order Forms:** The data transaction here is also fairly straightforward. Users indicate what product they want, how they intend to pay for it, and where the product should be sent. The web site builders should provide a clear and easy way to skip back to the web site to verify selections, and as a means of double-checking data before it is submitted.

- ❖ **Surveys:** Survey forms can be used as a way to try and determine more about one's audience than their ISPs and times of visit. The challenge in a survey is to try and present a variety of highly specific questions without cluttering the interface.

- ❖ **Search Interfaces:** As the web becomes larger, users need more sophisticated means of sifting through the content to find what they're looking for. A good search interface enables the user to enter a search query on a sliding scale of specificity. Users can search for a subject by setting parameters: searching for "pets" can mean "pets and dogs," "pets not dogs," or "pets or dogs." The second part of a good search interface is how the results are presented. The criteria that sort the results must be readily apparent.

NOTE | For full-color representations of the templates, access the CD-ROM that accompanies this book.

Figure 6_a_01

This is a basic example of a guestbook. The important items are set apart by the bold text, and the strong spaces between the different entries. Note also that each area for text input has some sort of explanatory text next to it.

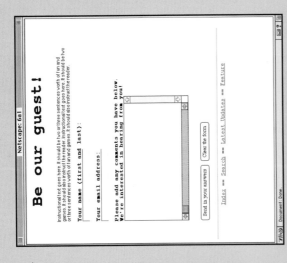

Figure 6_a_02

The different elements here are lined up along a strong vertical margin. This helps to pull the input elements out from the rest of the page and provides a visual sense of order. Another item to notice is that the entry text is in a different font than the explanatory text.

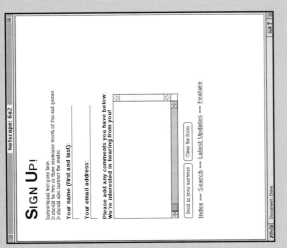

Figure 6_a_03

The center alignment of the different items in the form adds visual interest to a generic form. Notice that the fonts, while still clearly correlated to specific functions, are smaller, thus enabling the center eyeline to gather more visual emphasis.

Figure 6_a_04

This layout relies on subtle color shifts to set apart different question-and-answer sections. For the color to have the highest impact, a basic layout and generous whitespace between elements is important.

Figure 6_a_05

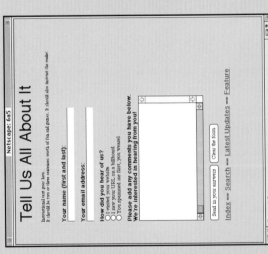

This layout precedes a two-page progression. Its basic composition and clear font-function correlation provide strong visual cues that will carry well across a few pages. Notice that information that the site provides—navigational cues and explanatory text—is provided in bold sans serif, and user-driven input is formatted in serif text.

Figure 6_a_06

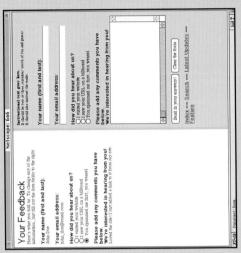

This is what appears after the user hits submit on the preceding page. Notice that the new content appears first—on the left—and that it's highlighted by means of a lighter background color. Aesthetic consistency between the two pages is maintained via similar layouts and consistent use of fonts for denoting different information.

Figure 6_b_01

This extremely basic registration form is both attractive and functional because of its strict margins. Note that all the data entry areas are set up within one table row, thus ensuring a strict margin. Another item to note: the radio button is used for a multiple choice option where there is only one desirable answer. Check boxes can perform the same function, but are more frequently used when the reader has the option of selecting more than one item in an array.

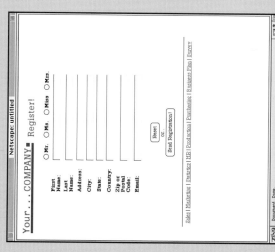

Figure 6_b_02

This page would appear after the user had submitted a registration form like the one shown in the preceding template. Note that this page serves one simple function: to let the user know that they had completed registration successfully. The layout is accordingly simple, and still contains header and navigation bar items that tie it into the registration form.

Figure 6_b_03

When a registration form becomes more complex, it's necessary to separate the requested information areas into related categories and to visually separate the category areas from each other. This enables you to add to or subtract from category areas as the need arises, and it enables the reader to negotiate the different parts of the form without confusion. Here, the different categories on the form are denoted by different background colors.

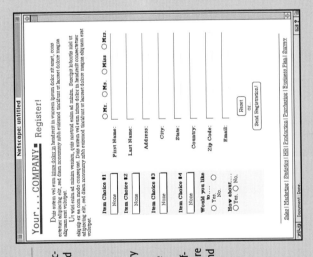

Figure 6_b_04

This counterpart page to the registration form maintains the color-category correlation. This page is slightly more information-rich than the preceding results page: not only does it tell the user the status of his registration, but it also enables the user to see what he filled in. This revision option is a welcome courtesy for most readers because online forms aren't as easily reviewed as forms that you have to fill out by hand.

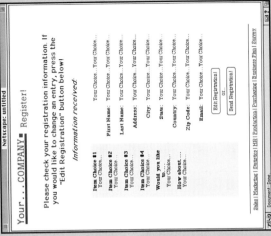

Figure 6_b_05

Here is an alternate layout for registration forms that include several different categories of information. A table is still used as the markup means for separating different categories of questions, but this table layout relies on strong vertical eyelines and space rather than color. If you want to avoid using table cell colors—which you may if your audience is comprised of users with low-end technology—this is a solid layout.

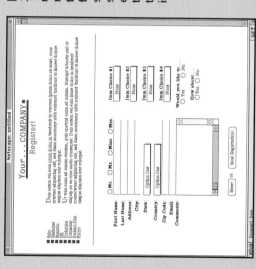

Figure 6_b_06

The error page is another necessary component in any registration process. It updates the reader on the success or failure of his efforts, and it should tell the reader what steps he needs to take to eliminate the error. Note that this layout relies on colored text to point out what element is missing for the reader.

Figure 6_b_07

This is the first page of a two-step registration form. The layout is clear in notifying the reader of that fact and in letting the reader know where they are in the registration process. Remember, registration forms online must be absolutely unambiguous. The person filling out the form doesn't have the luxury of being able to flip back and forth from page to page, so any and all navigation must be clean and consistent.

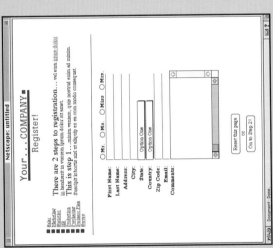

Figure 6_b_08

The second page of the registration form maintains visual continuity by providing navigation cues in the same places as the first registration page did, by maintaining the same layout, and by formatting the entry area with the same margins. Visual consistency helps the reader feel as though he is successfully navigating a multi-step process. If you find that you are unable to maintain visual consistency in your registration forms, you may want to reevaluate how you're organizing your data.

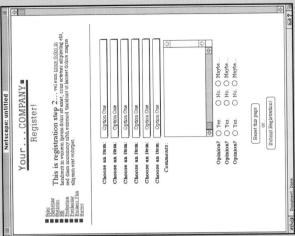

Figure 6_b_09

The results page for the two-page registration form displays all the results on one page but groups the results as two visually separate areas. This allows the reader to see the sum results of their entries and maintain some sense of the flow of questions—the reader can see what he filled out on page one and page two. Tying the results into the previous two pages—the same color and layout scheme.

Figure 6_b_10

A complex first page of a multipage registration can still be laid out cleanly and comprehensively. Note that the different question areas are strictly separated via strong horizontal and vertical strips of whitespace, and that the question formats differ sharply from section to section. Drawing visual distinctions is as important as drawing content-based distinctions. You may want to work closely with whoever is authoring the survey to ensure that you can achieve a strong correlation between the data-entry format and the intended function of the data query.

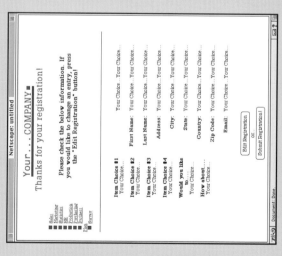

Figure 6_b_11

The complex layout continues into the second page of the registration form. Notice that the layout relies on a strong horizontal eyeline between the two different categories of question. This eyeline keeps the areas visually distinct and functionally separate.

Figure 6_b_12

The final confirmation page maintains several complex arrays of data by implementing a few simple layout strategies. Each section has a distinct column that it "owns" on the page. The data is smaller than the questions, thus allowing users to find out what they're looking at quickly, and the color corresponds to different data sections.

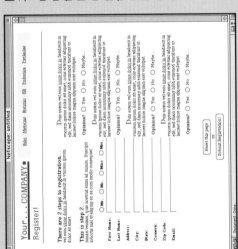

Figure 6_c_01

This is a good, basic layout for an order form. The different colors for the fields where numerical totals will be filled in do a good job of indicating to the reader that these areas are functionally different from the other parts of the order form. The color was fixed by tabling the entry form, setting each field as an individual table cell, and then changing the table cell colors as needed. Note that the table cell padding is set above zero, which allows the reader to see the background color. If the cell padding were zero, the data field would take all of it, thus canceling out any effect.

Figure 6_c_02

The colors in the data tags reflect the order form, which is a good way to ensure continuity between the order form and the user's choices. Note also that the layout is the same as the order form, further cementing the continuity.

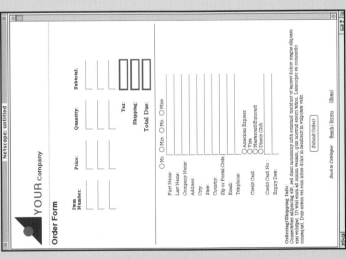

217

Figure 6_c_03

A different way of laying out order form information. Separate the two functionally different parts via layout and color—the ordering information runs vertically in a gray sidebar, while customer information is laid out more traditionally in the body of the document. This further reinforces the difference between the two areas' different font faces. You might consider a form like this if the customer information can be provided automatically on a repeat order.

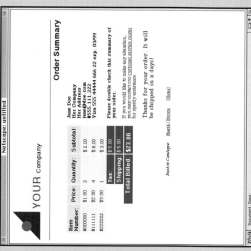

Figure 6_c_04

The color and layout separation are still sustained in the results page of the order form. Note that the strict layout was set up by tabling the order form results, then setting that table into a larger one formatting the page. This prevents having to utilize countless <COLSPAN> and <ROWSPAN> tags and enables you to focus on formatting the information as cleanly and modularly as possible.

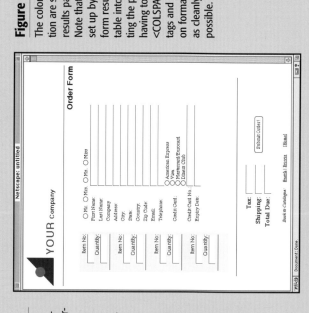

Figure 6_c_05

Strong horizontal eyelines and judicious use of color help set apart the different elements in this layout. This page avoids looking too blocky because of the center alignment.

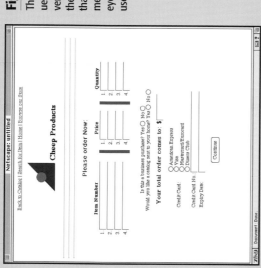

Figure 6_c_06

The center alignment continues and is reinforced by the vertical eyeline running down the center of the page. Note that the different form elements line up along the center eyeline as well. This is a good use of the <TD ALIGN> tag.

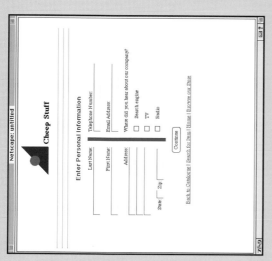

Figure 6_c_07

This is the results form from the previous two templates. It fits into the progression of pages by picking up the color scheme from the previous two templates, maintaining the center eyeline, and continuing the functional assignments to sans serif (site information) and serif fonts (page specific).

Figure 6_c_08

The layout on this page works so well because the two different lines that box in the form are clearly established. The horizontal line between the page beginning and the form does a good job of separating the site information from the interactive section, and the strong vertical eyeline down the form lines up and organizes all the disparate elements. Other items to note: strict use of sans serif fonts is used to guide the reader to information, and the use of color to visually separate different portions of information.

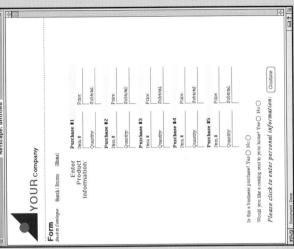

Figure 6_c_09

The same traits that made the previous layout successful—strong margins, visual separation of information in the entry form via color blocks, and the sans serif font as a directional font—are back for page two of the form.

Figure 6_c_10

The results page of the order form. Note that the strong vertical and horizontal line boxing in the form results from the rest of the page still maintaining the look and feel set up in the previous two pages. Two pages' worth of information is featured here, and it's separated into two parts by color use—the order form reflects the colors used to define the personal information is lined up according to the eyelines set out earlier.

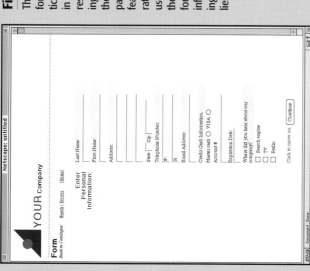

Figure 6_c_11

The magic of table tags. All the data fields make some sense because they're grouped spatially with strong vertical and horizontal eyelines—a nice way to use tables both for formatting purposes and functional purposes. The layout stays clean and uncluttered because the fonts are kept simple and color use is minimal.

Figure 6_c_12

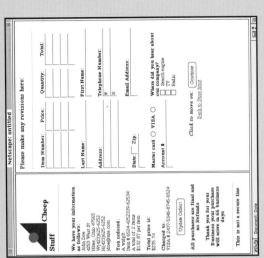

Frames perform a good information-path purpose. The information that the user entered is displayed on the left, with the same search interface available on the right, in case the user wants to make revisions. Notice that the two pages are tied together by the same color scheme.

Figure 6_d_01

This survey form takes up a minimal amount of space because every item in the array is featured as part of a pull-down menu. This option is a good way to save space if you have several items in a series, or if the items are particularly wordy.

Figure 6_d_02

The results format closely parallels the survey format. The similar formatting is important for maintaining visual and contextual continuity through a multipage user/server interaction. Note that a contrasting color was used to highlight the user answer, so users could easily find the data they provided to the web site.

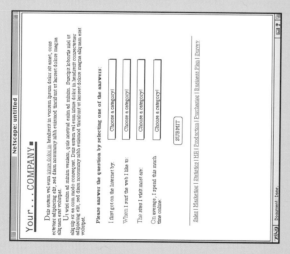

Figure 6_d_03

Color and space set apart this array of multiple choice questions. This layout works best with different colored table cells setting the content apart from the whitespace, but will also work functionally if the user is viewing it in any browser that supports tables. From a larger layout perspective, note that the survey area is set apart from the general page layout by four distinct blocks of whitespace.

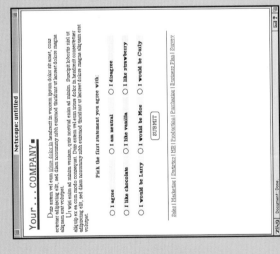

Figure 6_d_04

The accompanying answer form echoes the layout for the survey form in using table cell colors to set survey content apart from the rest of the page. The center alignment helps pull all the data in line with the results header and revision button.

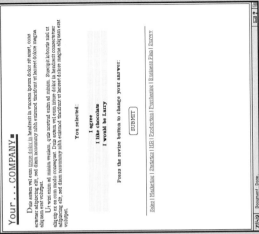

Figure 6_d_05

Text-heavy questions are separated from each other by liberal use of whitespace, and separated from the rest of the page by making the interactive area a distinctly different color. Other layout items that prevent this page from looking too clumped or boxy are that the strict left alignment within the survey area keeps the visual area clean and uncluttered, and the bold questions highlight the hierarchical category in which the data lives.

Figure 6_d_06

Note that the answers to the questions asked parallel the question format. This helps to maintain consistency by appropriating the visual cues that place content within a level of the site hierarchy. The contrasting color for the answers performs two functions: it ties into the web site color scheme, and it reinforces that the content—although on the same hierarchical level as the questions—is substantively different.

Figure 6_d_07

The two different question-asking formats are separated both spatially and via use of color. This enables you to group like types of queries—multiple choice, short-answer, and free form—together, and gives you larger conceptual sections around which to plan your layout. Specific details in this layout: parallel formatting for questions (bold subheading, plain text) and alignment maintain stylistic consistency through the different sections.

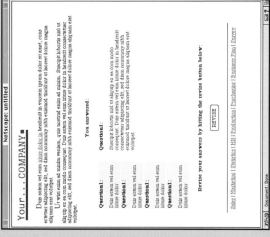

Figure 6_d_08

The two elements that tie this layout into the previous survey are the way that the formatting of the question and answer section parallels the formatting of the questions in the survey, and the arrangement of the answers parallels the way the questions were presented. As surveys get more complex, you may want to look into ways to save space displaying answers. Stacking answers on the left is one solution. Another might be to reduce font size until everything fits.

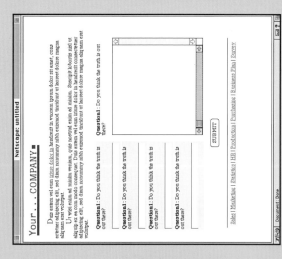

Figure 6_e_01

This layout works well because very few elements are in it, and the existing elements are set apart by space and layout boundaries. Note that site-wide layout conventions such as the heading and body text have a different alignment than the main purpose of the page—the search area. The search area is self-contained and the layout exercised within it—search choices and search tips—is restricted only to that area of the page.

Figure 6_e_02

This is the follow-up page to the preceding search interface. The results of the search look like a natural part of the web site because the layout is reflecting the site-wide traits (heading, alignment, same font conventions as the body text) as the web site—as opposed to looking like the search interface. One way to keep the web site looking like a cohesive product is to make sure that any results of user-directed activity visually and contextually tie into the rest of the web site.

Figure 6_e_03

The search interface is quite complex, so it's necessary to visually separate the functions the search engine can perform from each other and from the body text in the rest of the web page. The TABLE tag does a great job neatly partitioning everything and allowing some consistency with vertical and horizontal eyelines.

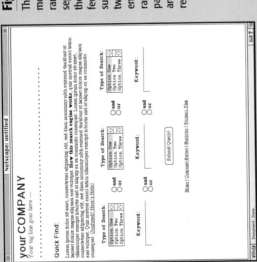

your COMPANY
Your tag line goes here —

Quick Find:

Lorem ipsum dolor sit amet, consectetuer adipiscing elit, sed diam nonummy nibh euismod tincidunt ut laoreet dolore magna aliquam erat volutpat. **How this search engine works**, quis nostrud exerci tation ullamcorper suscipit lobortis nisl ut aliquip ex ea commodo consequat. Lorem ipsum dolor sit amet, consectetuer adipiscing elit, sed diam nonummy nibh euismod tincidunt ut laoreet dolore magna aliquam erat volutpat. Quis nostrud exerci tation ullamcorper suscipit lobortis nisl ut aliquip ex ea commodo consequat. Continued! Here's Help!

Type of Search: Type of Search: Type of Search:
Option One   Option One   Option One
Option Two   Option Two   Option Two
Option Three   Option Three   Option Three

○ and   ○ and   ○ and
○ or   ○ or   ○ or

Keyword: **Keyword:**   **Keyword:**

[Submit Query!]

Home | Company Survey | Statistics | Business Plan

Figure 6_e_04

The results page is also a little more complex. The results are ranked by probability and separated by headers. Because the user had searched with a few more parameters, the results are also laid out to reflect two goals: to show the presence (or absence) of those parameters, and to draw a visual parallel between those results and the look and feel of the rest of the web site.

your COMPANY
Your tag line goes here —

Quick Find *Results:*

Best Bet:

Hit that matches your search criteria:
Lorem ipsum dolor sit amet, consectetuer adipiscing elit, sed diam nonummy nibh euismod tincidunt ut laoreet dolore magna aliquam erat volutpat. Lorem ipsum dolor sit amet, consectetuer adipiscing elit, sed diam nonummy nibh euismod tincidunt ut laoreet dolore magna aliquam erat volutpat.

Hit that matches your search criteria:
Lorem ipsum dolor sit amet, consectetuer adipiscing elit, sed diam nonummy nibh euismod tincidunt ut laoreet dolore magna aliquam erat volutpat. Lorem ipsum dolor sit amet, consectetuer adipiscing elit, sed diam nonummy nibh euismod tincidunt ut laoreet dolore magna aliquam erat volutpat.

Good Chance:

Hit that matches your search criteria:
Lorem ipsum dolor sit amet, consectetuer adipiscing elit, sed diam nonummy nibh euismod tincidunt ut laoreet dolore magna aliquam erat volutpat. Lorem ipsum dolor sit amet, consectetuer adipiscing elit, sed diam nonummy nibh euismod tincidunt ut laoreet dolore magna aliquam erat volutpat.

Hit that matches your search criteria:
Lorem ipsum dolor sit amet, consectetuer adipiscing elit, sed diam nonummy nibh euismod tincidunt ut laoreet dolore magna aliquam erat volutpat. Lorem ipsum dolor sit amet, consectetuer adipiscing elit, sed diam nonummy nibh euismod tincidunt ut laoreet dolore magna aliquam erat volutpat.

Hit that matches your search criteria:
Lorem ipsum dolor sit amet, consectetuer adipiscing elit, sed diam nonummy nibh euismod tincidunt ut laoreet dolore magna aliquam erat volutpat. Lorem ipsum dolor sit amet, consectetuer adipiscing elit, sed diam nonummy nibh euismod tincidunt ut laoreet dolore magna aliquam erat volutpat.

It's a long shot:

Hit that matches your search criteria:
Lorem ipsum dolor sit amet, consectetuer adipiscing elit, sed diam nonummy nibh euismod tincidunt ut laoreet dolore magna aliquam erat volutpat. Lorem ipsum dolor sit amet, consectetuer adipiscing elit, sed diam nonummy nibh euismod tincidunt ut laoreet dolore magna aliquam erat volutpat.

Hit that matches your search criteria:
Lorem ipsum dolor sit amet, consectetuer adipiscing elit, sed diam nonummy nibh euismod tincidunt ut laoreet dolore magna aliquam erat volutpat. Lorem ipsum dolor sit amet, consectetuer adipiscing elit, sed diam nonummy nibh euismod tincidunt ut laoreet dolore magna aliquam erat volutpat.

[Next 10 Results | New Search]

Home | Company Survey | Statistics | Business Plan

Figure 6_e_05

If the site's search feature is a tool for site-wide use rather than web-wide use, part of the challenge of designing a search page is trying to convey the search functionality without aesthetically separating it from the rest of the site. The search area in this layout is set apart by a strong horizontal block of whitespace, and all the elements within the search area are lined up along a center eyepath. Note that the "box" that is pulled into the layout by the heading at the top and the navigation bar at the bottom.

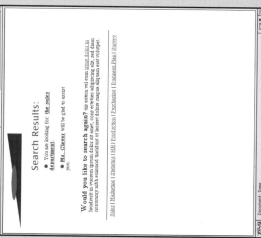

Figure 6_e_06

These are the search results for the preceding sample's interface. The tie-in to the prior layout is the color scheme. The formatting for the keyword instructions in the preceding template match the formatting for the keyword results in this one. The heading and navigation bars provide the same box format that you saw in the search interface. This layout helps to maintain continuity between user action and server results.

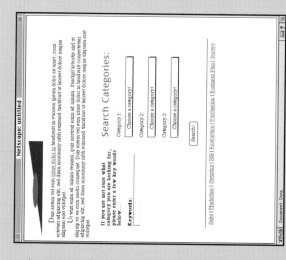

Figure 6_e_07

This is a more complex search interface, with a number of choices. The strategy here was to box everything into a layout that could carry from page to page across the site, then line up all the options within strict vertical margins.

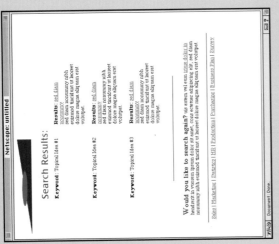

Figure 6_e_08

The results page echoes the arrangement of the search options on the preceding page. Keyword results are on the left, and longer results are on the right. Notice that the strict horizontal and vertical eyelines are still in evidence, thus maintaining layout continuity between the search interface and the results page.

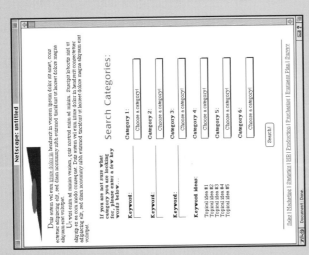

Figure 6_e_09

The search interface is clearly separated from the rest of the layout via the use of colored table cells. The left and right margins are set in farther than the rest of the page, thus performing two different functions: setting the search area aside as something functionally distinct, and ensuring that the color block doesn't overwhelm the rest of the screen.

Figure 6_e_10

This layout is composed of two parts—the results section, which continues the same spatial scheme and palette as the search interface, and a second, reduced interface. The two main reasons why this search section looks different from the main search interface are that it is meant for refining a previous search, not replicating the process, and it is meant to look functionally distinct from the search results listed above.

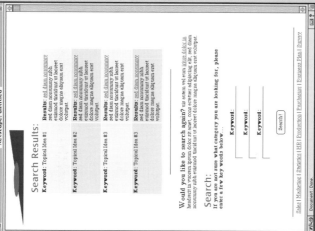

Figure 6_e_11

A customizable search interface cuts down on the amount of screen real estate the search interface requires. This is good if you're trying to stick to one-screen layouts. Notice that the search topics are set apart from the categories via color blocks, thus implying that the two columns serve distinctly different functions.

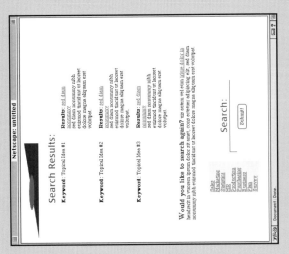

Figure 6_e_12

The search interface is duplicated again at the bottom of the page. This is a much different functional strategy than the previous one discussed. This layout repetition invites the reader to begin a new search from scratch.

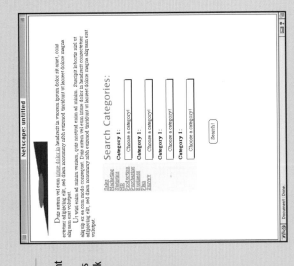

Figure 6_e_13

Search tips are pulled into sharp focus via the use of color. Note that the data generated—the top keywords—is a function that will rely on server feedback and response, rather than something hardcoded into the layout. Another item to notice in the layout is that the keyword search function has a visually separate look from the rest of the search interface, thus cueing the reader into its effectiveness.

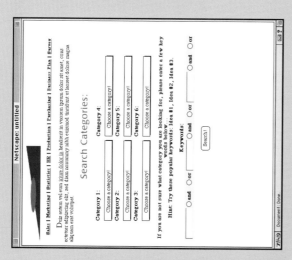

Figure 6_e_14

The results page for the previous search interface continues to use color to highlight relevant information. Here, it's reinforcing the connection between user input and server results. The repeated search interface is also keyword-focused and reiterates the use of color-as-search-cue, thus reinforcing to the reader that the keyword search is the most effective.

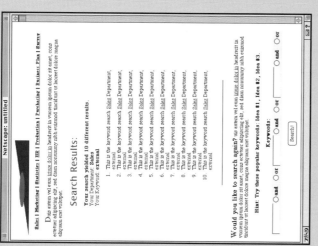

Figure 6_e_15

This template takes advantage of a more intricate use of color to set apart different functions in the layout. Each search category is assigned its own color. This could come in handy if the user is going to be searching a web site with several different "channels" and is likely to get results from each channel.

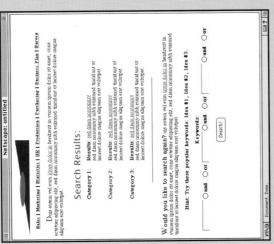

Figure 6_e_16

The color scheme introduced in the preceding template is reiterated in the results layout. This is a good strategy if you anticipate the search results being long because the color provides a handy visual code to which criteria the results are meeting.

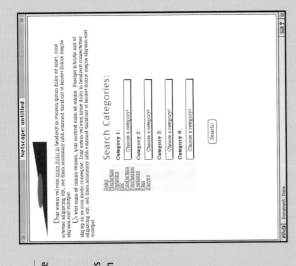

CHAPTER 7

Multifunctional Sites

What this chapter covers:

- ❖ What Is a Multifunctional Site?
- ❖ Integrating All the Functional Parts into One Site
- ❖ Maintaining Look and Feel Across the Site
- ❖ Templates for:
  - ◆ Collegiate Course Web Sites
  - ◆ Frames-Based Pedagogical Web Sites
  - ◆ Product Catalogs

What Is a Multifunctional Site?

As Chapter 6, "Forms," demonstrated, web sites are comprised of several different types of data transactions. Some are user-driven, such as selecting and reading news articles. Some require a give-and-take between the user and the site, such as running a search for specific news articles. Most readers conduct both types of data transactions when they visit a site, especially if they're visiting for information-gathering purposes.

Web sites are also comprised of several different types of information. A corporate web site may have an area devoted exclusively to press releases, another covering its financial dealings, and a third cataloging its products. Each area should use hypertext and online markup to best present the content; but how do you maintain a standard look-and-feel across the site? Do you want to?

This chapter looks at ways to pull together all the different types of templates in the previous chapters. You'll learn about strategies for finding common links between different content types and information transactions, and how to build a site that can convey different types of information to your readers, while maintaining the specificity of each part.

Integrating All the Functional Parts into One Site

Before you can outline a strategy for integrating all the parts of a web site into a whole, you need to be able to identify what those parts are, and how they relate to each other. The first question you should ask (not coincidentally, it's also the biggest) is what kind of information will be moving between the reader and your site?

Identifying the nature of the information will help you to determine what the common denominator is within every subsection of the web site. After you've identified what the common denominator is, you can decide how to convey it visually, how to carry it across the sections, and to what level you need to carry it within each section.

Assume, for example, that you are building a web site for a small college. The public information officer you're working with has specified that the web site must provide information in distinct parts. Before you do anything, you need to determine the nature of data transactions that will occur at this site. What kind of information is moving from web site to user? What kind of information is moving from the user to the web site? In the college information example, you'd encounter the following:

❖ **College brochure:** A reader is looking for general information about the school; he may not have a specific reason for being on the site.

❖ **Visitation schedules and registration:** A few data transactions are here. An interested reader is looking for specific information and is acting on that information by registering for a visit.

❖ **Research press releases:** A reporter or student who is looking for specific updates is looking for information from the school.

❖ **Class schedules:** A student is actively seeking information from the school. This is targeted more toward an internal audience than an external one.

❖ **Course registrations:** A student is entering information in exchange for class scheduling. This is targeted more toward an internal audience than an external one.

❖ **Course descriptions:** A student or a possible student is looking for reference information.

❖ **A student directory:** Casual information seeking: this is targeted more toward an internal audience than an external one.

❖ **Departmental home pages:** A student, potential student, or researcher gathering background material. This is built for a specific audience, but not necessarily an internal one.

Looking at the different data transactions in the various parts of the college information site, a few noticeable factors are:

❖ Internal audience versus external audience

❖ Public audience versus community audience

❖ Actively sought data versus passively encountered data

The best way to proceed might be to split the site into two different areas: internal audience and external audience. The following step-by-step procedure illustrates how you can accomplish this.

1. Create a logical external/internal division for the site. The external part of the web site showcases the school as a whole—brochures, visiting schedules, and registration. The internal part of the web site focuses on information the student community actively seeks, such as class schedules, course descriptions, and registration. In addition, the internal part addresses information that people involved with, or interested in, the academic community will seek out, such as press releases and departmental home pages.

2. Link the external and internal parts of the site while maintaining a clear division between their functionality. One way to do this might be to maintain similar layout styles across the top pages of each section, but make the color schemes radically different. Another method might be to incorporate a clear visual cue on the navigation bar that separates the external section of the web site from the internal one.

3. Incorporate different types of data transactions within the separate sections on the site. Of course, you'll also need to visually distinguish these transactions without making the site seem crowded or overwhelming. One way you can do this is to pare down what you offer on navigation bars or the table of contents. This is not hiding the information from a reader, it's prioritizing the data.

4. Provide a logical navigation tool to the external and internal parts of the site. One strategy for dealing with the section-specific hierarchies of information would be to limit what appears on the navigation bars at different levels of the site. The index page of the course catalog pages, for example, would show links to the class schedules and registration sections, but individual course page navigation bars would refer to other departments, and then back up to the course catalog home. Representing specific levels of information reinforces the feeling of the section as a discrete unit within a larger whole—which is desirable if you're pulling together several functionally different sections into a larger whole. The design elements are still the same: navigation bar, consistent layout, and clear hierarchy of information. The only added consideration is how these elements will mesh with site-wide elements.

Maintaining Look and Feel Across the Site

Multifunctional sites are the web projects where the sharpest distinction between the following two design considerations are found:

- ❖ Web page design
- ❖ Web site design

To clarify, *web page design* focuses on the visual layout and aesthetics of a web page, such as aligning elements, setting browser width, or otherwise determining what will make the web page as aesthetically pleasing as possible. *Web site design* focuses on building a total product regarding visual cues that act as guides for the reader, what sort of information hierarchy will be set up and how that will be reflected in the site, and what design elements need to be kept constant.

Web page design can be a valuable part of the site design process, but it is not a substitute. A site is more than its look. A site must also provide a comprehensive organizational pattern embodied in the file tree and the visual equivalent of a place for everything and everything in its place. Some design issues you will always have to consider, such as maintaining a clean eyepath through a web page, keeping the color scheme consistent, and balancing font faces with the words they spell. The design of a page, however, is subordinate to that of the entire site. The following sections discuss the most important elements to consider when designing a multifunctional site.

Color

Color is an invaluable tool for establishing consistent design traits or to indicate a specific section. You can set up a color scheme that works across the entire site (gray text, blue links, and pine-green expired links) or set up a color key to indicate where a user is on the site, such as red headlines to indicate news releases, blue headlines to indicate archived material, and orange headlines to indicate help pages. Or, different chapters of a paper have different background colors. The key is to use color systematically.

Text

Visual cues via text size, attribute, or font can create and maintain an information hierarchy. You can also exploit text size/fonts to create a site-specific typographic trademark. Text should also correlate to the type of content—this is a functional rule-of-thumb for site design.

Page Size and Format

Implementing page size and format in a site does not mean to set your browser to the width of this line. This means determining what the eyeline is in your layout and how to maintain that across many different pages and over several different computer platforms. This means figuring out how large or how small web page files are in relation to each other—do you want a long series of rapidly-loading files, or a few longer files?

Information Hierarchy

You already know the importance of sorting out your content by its function and its relative importance to each other, for example, picture captions and story headlines carry different weight relative to the text of an article, and different weight relative to each other. Now ask yourself if this information hierarchy is applicable across the entire site, from survey forms to search pages to financial reports, or is this information hierarchy tailored to a particular type of section? If the latter is the case, what elements can you use to bridge to other parts of the site? What level of the information hierarchy do you want to use to tie the sections together on the navigation bar?

Examples of Multifunctional Sites

The following examples illustrate sites where design and structure tie web pages with several different purposes into a comprehensive site.

 NOTE For full-color representations of the templates, access the CD-ROM that accompanies this book.

Figure 7_a_01

As an entry page, this page sets the tone for the rest of the site. It will establish the visual cues that alert the reader to the different types of information categories within the entire site. This page does that by establishing a symbol system in the top-right corner: each section of the site has a bullet (small graphic) and color that are unique to that topic. In addition, a clear functional division is established with different font faces—sans serif fonts are used to cue the reader into site-wide organization or navigation, and the serif fonts present content.

Netscape: 7_a_01

Course Website...... ● **Class Notes ~** **Test!** **Tutorial*** **Syllabus~**

Course Title: Learning New Stuff
Course Number: learn101
Date: 1/1/2000 - 2/1/2000
Instructor: Clever Girl

- **Plan for Week 1:**
Suscipit lobortis nisl ut aliquip ex ea com modo consequat. Duis autem vel eum iriure dolor in hendrerit consectetuer adipiscing elit, sed diam nonummy nibh euismod tincidunt ut laoreet dolore magna aliquam erat volutpat. Ut wisi enim ad minim veniam, quis nostrud exerci tation.

- **Plan for Week 2:**
Suscipit lobortis nisl ut aliquip ex ea com modo consequat. Duis autem vel eum iriure dolor in hendrerit consectetuer adipiscing elit, sed diam nonummy nibh euismod tincidunt ut laoreet dolore magna aliquam erat volutpat. Ut wisi enim ad minim veniam, quis nostrud exerci tation.

- **Plan for Week 3:**
Suscipit lobortis nisl ut aliquip ex ea com modo consequat. Duis autem vel eum iriure dolor in hendrerit consectetuer adipiscing elit, sed diam nonummy nibh euismod tincidunt ut laoreet dolore magna aliquam erat volutpat. Ut wisi enim ad minim veniam, quis nostrud exerci tation.

- **Plan for Week 4:**
Suscipit lobortis nisl ut aliquip ex ea com modo consequat. Duis autem vel eum iriure dolor in hendrerit consectetuer adipiscing elit, sed diam nonummy nibh euismod tincidunt ut laoreet dolore magna aliquam erat volutpat. Ut wisi enim ad minim veniam, quis nostrud exerci tation.

Back to Course Listing   Previous Course   Next Course   Home

Document: Done.

Figure 7_a_02

This layout handles a text-heavy page with several different layout tricks. Content is divided along strong horizontal eyelines. This technique allows the user to be able to page up or down without chopping the content—or the reader's stream of thought. Content abstracts are also indented from the main body of the text, thus enabling the reader to distinguish between specific types of data in each content segment.

Netscape: 7_a_02

Course Website...... ● **Tutorial*** **Test!** **Class Notes~** **Syllabus~**

Course Title: Learning New Stuff
Course Number: learn101
Date: 1/1/2000 - 2/1/2000
Instructor: Clever Girl
Previous Week's Class Notes/Next Week's Class Notes

Suscipit lobortis nisl ut aliquip ex ea com modo consequat. Duis autem vel eum iriure dolor in hendrerit consectetuer adipiscing elit, sed diam nonummy nibh euismod tincidunt ut laoreet dolore magna aliquam erat volutpat. Ut wisi enim ad minim veniam, quis nostrud exerci tation.

Lorem ipsum dolor sit amet
Duis autem vel eum iriure dolor in hendrerit in vu

Lorem ipsum dolor sit amet, consectetuer adipiscing elit, sed diam nonummy nibh euismod tincidunt ut laoreet dolore magna aliquam erat volutpat. Ut wisi enim ad minim veniam, quis nostrud exerci tation.

Exerci Tation Ullamcorper:
Suscipit lobortis nisl ut aliquip ex ea com modo consequat. Duis autem vel eum iriure dolor in hendrerit consectetuer adipiscing elit, sed diam nonummy nibh euismod tincidunt ut laoreet dolore magna aliquam erat volutpat. Ut wisi enim ad minim veniam, quis nostrud exerci tation. Lemscoper ex ea commodo consequat. Duis autem vel eum iriure dolor in hendrerit in vulputate velit. consectetuer adipiscing elit, sed diam nonummy nibh euismod tincidunt ut laoreet dolore magna aliquam erat volutpat. Conuec teruer adipiscing elit, sed diam nonummy nibh euismod tincidunt ut laoreet dolore magna aliquam erat volutpat.

Lorem ipsum dolor sit amet
Duis autem vel eum iriure dolor in hendrerit in vu

Lorem ipsum dolor sit amet, consectetuer adipiscing elit, sed diam nonummy nibh euismod tincidunt ut laoreet dolore magna aliquam erat volutpat. Ut wisi enim ad minim veniam, quis nostrud exerci tation.

Exerci Tation Ullamcorper:
Suscipit lobortis nisl ut aliquip ex ea com modo consequat. Duis autem vel eum iriure dolor in hendrerit consectetuer adipiscing elit, sed diam nonummy nibh euismod tincidunt ut laoreet dolore magna aliquam erat volutpat. Ut wisi enim ad minim veniam, quis nostrud exerci tation. Lemscoper ex ea commodo consequat. Duis autem vel eum iriure dolor in hendrerit in vulputate velit. consectetuer adipiscing elit, sed diam nonummy nibh euismod tincidunt ut laoreet dolore magna aliquam erat volutpat. Conuec teruer adipiscing elit, sed diam nonummy nibh euismod tincidunt ut laoreet dolore magna aliquam erat volutpat.

Lorem ipsum dolor sit amet
Duis autem vel eum iriure dolor in hendrerit in vu

Lorem ipsum dolor sit amet, consectetuer adipiscing elit, sed diam nonummy nibh euismod tincidunt ut laoreet dolore magna aliquam erat volutpat. Ut wisi enim ad minim veniam, quis nostrud exerci tation.

Exerci Tation Ullamcorper:
Suscipit lobortis nisl ut aliquip ex ea com modo consequat. Duis autem vel eum iriure dolor in hendrerit consectetuer adipiscing elit, sed diam nonummy nibh euismod tincidunt ut laoreet dolore magna aliquam erat volutpat. Ut wisi enim ad minim veniam, quis nostrud exerci tation. Lemscoper ex ea commodo consequat. Duis autem vel eum iriure dolor in hendrerit in vulputate velit. consectetuer adipiscing elit, sed diam nonummy nibh euismod tincidunt ut laoreet dolore magna aliquam erat volutpat. Conuec teruer adipiscing elit, sed diam nonummy nibh euismod tincidunt ut laoreet dolore magna

Back to Course Listing   Previous Course   Next Course   Home

Document: Done.

Figure 7_a_03

The different information in this layout is distinguished by different font sizes, faces, and weight. Note that the organization of the site-wide information is still established and maintained by the sans serif fonts, and that the content is sorted into different categories via bold headings and plain text.

Figure 7_a_04

The challenge of incorporating instructional images into a layout is to try and make sure that the image gets presented well (for maximum comprehension) without throwing off the rest of the layout. Here, the images are lined up and presented as part of a larger chunk of information. These chunks are set apart visually by strong horizontal eyelines and section heads.

COLLEGIATE COURSE WEB SITES

241

Figure 7_a_05

Notice that the test questions are visually sorted and separated by the signal—the exclamation point—that denotes the "test" section of the web site. This use of signal performs two functions. It reinforces the visual navigation system set up by the four signals at the top of each page, and it provides a way to group each question and answer section together.

Figure 7_a_06

The counterpart page to the test questions continues the same visual signals as the previous quiz page. The design further reinforces the content category—tests—by making each answer heading the same color as the exclamation point symbol.

Figure 7_a_07

Different typographic characteristics help to visually organize the information, but the real key to successfully setting apart different types of information lies in the way space and margins are used. Note that each segment of content is aligned and indented from its heading.

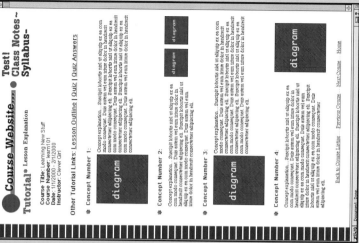

Figure 7_a_08

Tables are used to align and group text and images. Although a number of aesthetic benefits to doing this exist—clear and consistent vertical and horizontal eyelines are established—the primary reason for sorting the information this way is to group related items in a way that makes sense contextually and visually.

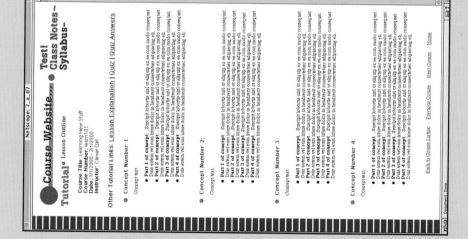

Figure 7_a_09

The different fonts used in this design set apart the page headings, the questions, and the answers. These visual cues are important if the page is to be one in a successive series—you need to establish a way to tell the reader when items of information across several web pages are related.

Figure 7_a_10

The typographic cues established in the preceding template are continued here. Because this page is always going to appear as part of a linear series, it's important to maintain the same typographic conventions and visual arrangement of elements that may be related. Here, that's practiced by the quiz answers appearing in the same type style as the questions, and in the same layout.

Figure 7_b_01

This layout continues with many of the same features that the previous section highlighted. There's a consistent symbol and color assigned to each section, and the layout for each page has strong vertical eyelines. Notice that increased priority is given to navigation. Because this web site contains a lot of information specific to one topic (in this case a course) but is still part of a larger site, the frame enables the user to switch web site levels quickly without getting lost.

Figure 7_b_02

This frames setup allows the user two different means of navigation. The left frame allows the user to move from a section index page to specific items within that subsite. The bottom frame allows the user to move from section to section within the entire site.

Figure 7_b_03

This is an example of how a multiple framed layout handles a text-heavy page. Notice that the other pages allow plenty of whitespace, thus preventing the text-heavy page form looking cluttered. If you're going to design a page with frames, it's important to consider how each file within a frame will affect the other files with which it is displayed.

Figure 7_b_04

The primary frame here relies heavily on illustrative images. Ensuring that the image-heavy page layout still maintains a clean and coherent layout without distracting from the overall frame layout is the biggest challenge. In this layout, it's done by scaling back the sizes of the images and boxing the content into a strictly-sized table, ensuring that the visually-packed content page does not distract from the rest of the layout.

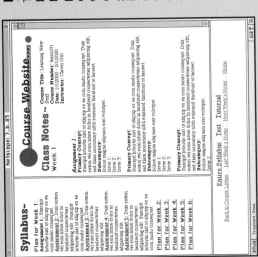

Figure 7_b_05

This is a great use of frames to illustrate the logical flow of information—the quiz is on the left and the answers are on the right. It's a safe bet that most of your readers are used to reading information left-to-right, so this layout reinforces that practice.

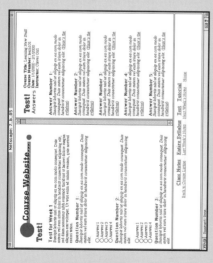

Figure 7_b_06

A different section of the web site is highlighted in this example. This shows how the different sections of a web site can maintain a visual identity and still seamlessly fit into an entire site. The trick is to maintain consistent layouts through the site and rely on a visual code to cue the reader. The color/symbol code does the trick here, signaling the reader that they are in a distinct section, but the font/data properties and overall layout remain the same.

Figure 7_b_07

The challenge of incorporating instructional images into a layout is to try and make sure that the image gets presented well (for maximum comprehension) without throwing off the rest of the layout. In this template, the images are presented as part of a larger section of information. These sections are set apart visually by strong horizontal eyelines and section heads.

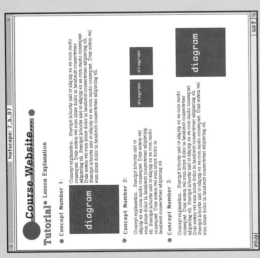

Figure 7_b_08

The different fonts used in this design set apart the page headings, the questions, and the answers. These visual cues are important if the page is to be one in a successive series—you need to establish a way to tell the reader when items of information across several web pages are related.

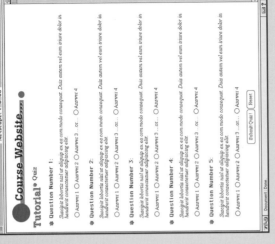

Figure 7_b_09

The typographic cues established in the preceding template are continued here. Because this page is always going to appear as part of a linear series, it's important to maintain the same typographic conventions and visual arrangement of elements that may be related. Here, that's practiced by the quiz answers appearing in the same type style as the questions, and in the same layout.

Netscape: 7_b_09

● Course Website... ●

Tutorial Quiz Answers

✦ **Answer Number 1:**

Suscipit lobortis nisl ut aliquip ex ea com modo consequat. Duis autem vel eum iriure dolor in hendrerit consectetuer adipiscing elit.

✦ **Answer Number 2:**

Suscipit lobortis nisl ut aliquip ex ea com modo consequat. Duis autem vel eum iriure dolor in hendrerit consectetuer adipiscing elit.

✦ **Answer Number 3:**

Suscipit lobortis nisl ut aliquip ex ea com modo consequat. Duis autem vel eum iriure dolor in hendrerit consectetuer adipiscing elit.

✦ **Answer Number 4:**

Suscipit lobortis nisl ut aliquip ex ea com modo consequat. Duis autem vel eum iriure dolor in hendrerit consectetuer adipiscing elit.

✦ **Answer Number 5:**

Suscipit lobortis nisl ut aliquip ex ea com modo consequat. Duis autem vel eum iriure dolor in hendrerit consectetuer adipiscing elit.

Document: Done

PRODUCT CATALOGS

Scheme 1

Figure 7_c_01

This design illustrates first-hand the flexibility that the use of a table may provide in presenting data. Note how varying the table cells produced a honeycomb effect and broke out of the blockiness that some tables have. To keep the information from overwhelming the user, color and spacing partitioned the portions of text.

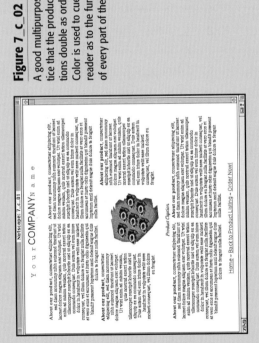

Figure 7_c_02

A good multipurpose site: notice that the product descriptions double as order forms. Color is used to cue the reader as to the functionality of every part of the page.

Figure 7_c_03

Another clean and uncluttered form. Don't be afraid to apply text-level tags like <TABLE> and all its attributes, and text attributes like <FONT> and <SIZE>. Presenting the information clearly and attractively should be an especially high priority on order forms.

251

Figure 7_d_01

As you can see in templates 7_d_01 through 7_d_03, frames enable the company to put up a detailed product page and still display the product listing. This is a good way to include READMEs for software, directions to a particular event (assuming events are what you're trying to see), or partitioning content-level information from site-level information. Frames can also be the one way that you ensure continuity across the site—one navigation frame on the left can tie together an extensive product sheet, a layout of products, and an order form—three different types of information that must be shown to be related. The web is a rapid-read medium—use visual shortcuts wherever possible.

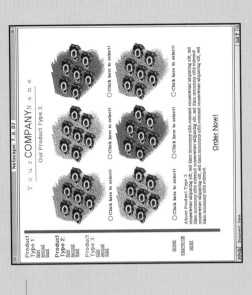

Figure 7_d_02

Figure 7_d_03

PRODUCT CATALOGS

Scheme 3

Figure 7_e_01

This layout works because it's extremely noncluttered and has a strong vertical eyeline in the center. The nonclutter includes only four items, formatted cleanly: the order head, the order form, a brief directions slug, and the submit button. The strong vertical eyeline was accomplished by exploiting <TD VALIGN> and <TD ALIGN> table tags. Remember that you can include text-level attributes within <FORM> tags.

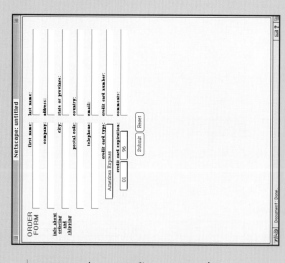

Figure 7_e_02

The closely aligned, neatly boxed layout has two technical points going for it. It can fit into one screen, and it's easily degradable to HTML 2.0. This ensures that our fictitious vendor reaches as many people as possible.

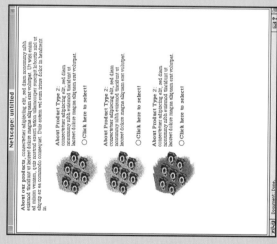

Figure 7_e_03

Another clean and non-browser-specific layout. Note that the vertical layout enables you to present more information and avoid looking cluttered. This is because of the strong vertical lines drawn by the whitespace.

Figure 7_e_04

The previous layout, flipped 180 degrees. This will work if your product list has a number of images that are fairly small and uniform in number—this way, you don't have to worry about a small browser window cutting the images. The reason that you'd adopt a layout like this is that the ordering information is the first thing the reader sees.

PRODUCT CATALOGS
Scheme 3

Figure 7_e_05

The beauty of this layout is that it enables you to swap in different functional parts and still maintain stylistic consistency through the rest of the site. This is accomplished by restricting the color choices to two or three basic hues that carry across all the pages, maintaining the same clean lines from section to section and clearly separating functional frame parts.

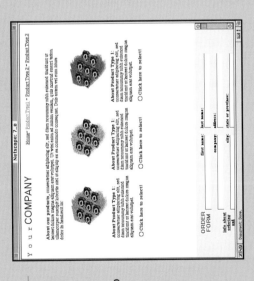

CHAPTER 8

Alternatives to HTML Templates

What this chapter covers:

- ❖ Second-Generation Web Site Development: What Is It?
- ❖ Dynamic HTML
- ❖ Style Sheets
- ❖ Layers
- ❖ Virtual Includes/Server-Side Includes
- ❖ CGI-Bin Scripting

Second-Generation Web Site Development: What Is It?

The majority of this book concentrates on designing and building first-generation web sites. For the sake of argument, *first-generation* means the first web site that reflects a concerted information tree and interface strategy. *Second-generation* refers to the next iteration in a web site's development.

A second-generation web site is one that is designed and built to utilize the most current web-specific technology. A second-generation web site might rely on increasing automation, instead of dropping text into static templates. Second-generation web site producers use tools that pull content from a database and push it through page formats generated on-the-fly. Second-generation web sites might shift the updating time frames—instead of pushing new content live once a day the web producers post new content once an hour—subsequently forcing web producers to look at content and presentation in a whole new way.

A second-generation web site does two things. It builds a dynamic, expanding product and treats every part within the product as a discrete object. In plain language, your first-generation web site could have been thought of as a book without bindings—each page a flat file with elements that pulled it into the idea of a site as a whole. Your second-generation web site is better thought of as a lego project. Each lego has its own individual properties: shape, color, and number of pegs. You can build different things with different combinations of legos.

Before this metaphor gets too tedious, let's move it over to your second-generation web site. On a first-generation web site, a typical page might have a navigation bar, a chunk of content, a list of related links, and a logo that must be on every web page. You established site consistency with page layouts, color schemes, and navigation devices. Looking at the four page elements in the context of a second-generation web site, you have the items discussed in table 8.1.

Table 8.1　Web Site Elements and Their Attributes

Element	Attribute
Logo	Visual, style, fixed site identity
Body Copy	Content, timely information, specific to query or date
Navigation Bar	Site-wide information, visual, style
Related Links	Side-wide information, timely information

The key to building a second- (or third-, or fourth-) generation web site is to look at the different elements in a "big picture" sort of way. Focus on *why* they came into existence, rather than what they currently do.

All these elements are on the page for some reason; the reasons are listed in the attributes column. When you go to build the second iteration of your site, ask if the *reason* still applies to the web site, as opposed to the object that carries the reason out.

The next step, to determine the best possible way, is to translate that reason into a web site element.

If your goal is to emphasize the interconnectedness of your web site's content, you could move from a group of related links to frames that load the actual interconnected content. If your goal is to provide a constant navigation device, you could try a JavaScripted toolbar that sits on the desktop apart from the site. The point is that you don't have to always carry out the functions in the same way that you did previously.

This is not to say that you should completely redo the site—your readership might rely on the way you've organized your content and the visual cues that you've set up to organize the site. But you should examine the different functions you want your web site to have, and plot the best way to implement those functions.

Given the rapidly evolving state of web scripting languages, web server software, web surfing tools, and the hardware that drives the entire industry, the best way to implement your web site might change.

The aim of this chapter is to introduce you to some of the second-generation techniques for building, maintaining, or remodeling a large-scale web site. This chapter is meant to whet your interest and demonstrate what's coming up—or already happening—in large-scale web site design.

Dynamic HTML

HTML was developed as a way to visually represent information; the visual lexicon it set up assumed every item on the page had a functional purpose. If you look at the specifications for early HTML, you'll see that every visual variation was grounded in some sort of functional rationale. Headings had seven different sizes to correspond with the levels in an outline-based hierarchy, lists could be ordered by number or unordered if the numbering scheme wasn't relevant, items could be emphasized or cited (not bolded or italicized).

The foundation for design was in place—the idea that every item in a layout ought to serve a function. The execution was a little less than aesthetically refined. Some folks have snidely pointed out that the web was built by and for physicists, implying that physicists have no sense of design.

This assertion isn't true. The people who developed HTML were concerned with presenting information in a visually recognizable way, which is exactly what design is supposed to do. The early design bias was toward hierarchical information representation, not widely variable visual information representation.

Over the past few years, HTML implementation has been pulled in two different directions. One camp favors structural representation of information. In this camp, the best web pages are those that convey information contained within the standard structural specifications because they convey proscribed information about an item. The other group argues that HTML offers a limited range of ways to present information visually, and HTML hacks are necessary to create functional interfaces. Most web design walks a line between the two arguments. Many of the templates in this book do just that.

Recently, HTML began to return to its structural beginnings. This does not mean that we're returning to the age of gray backgrounds and muddy purple links. Recent developments in HTML 3.2 and the soon-to-be-released versions of Netscape 4.0 and Microsoft Internet Explorer 4.0 will enable web site builders to write HTML that explicitly addresses form without sacrificing function.

The first new development is Dynamic HTML. Microsoft has trademarked the all-caps phrase, so let's discuss this first.

The most significant difference between dynamic HTML and Dynamic HTML is that the latter is Microsoft's phrase describing an HTML-driven way to change web page content, and the former is the general phrase naming the same processes.

As specified by Microsoft, Dynamic HTML is an object-oriented way of writing HTML. It is comprised of three distinct parts:

❖ **W3C HTML 3.2 Standards:** The W3C is the World Wide Web Consortium. This group develops the common specifications for the web's technical architecture (http protocol, for example) and user interface. HTML falls within the user interface category. The W3C defines precisely what each HTML tag will do within a document, what sort of attributes the tag will have, and what informational function it serves (if any).

❖ **Cascading Style Sheets (CSS) 1.0:** This is the W3 specification for a new approach to controlling web page appearance. Cascading Style Sheets, which are explained in detail in just a few paragraphs, are a way to set up a lot of really precise presentational elements for your content—font face, color, point size, for example—and have those same styles apply across documents on your site. Better yet, style sheets will allow you more control over how your pages will appear on anyone's browser.

❖ **Microsoft's Document Object Model:** This is a set of specifications Microsoft has developed to translate the HTML tags that you know and love into objects that can handle events. Translated into English, this means that a given tag in HTML no longer just tells the browser "put it there." It can also say, "put it there, until someone mouses over it, and then put it somewhere else." This doesn't mean that HTML has gone random on you—it just means that Microsoft is proposing a model for making HTML easier to read and react to from a script's point of view.

This tripartite model provides you with a way to manipulate your web page in new ways. You can change the look and feel of the headlines across all your pages with a line in a style sheet, and you can attach events (things happening with or to content on a page) to any element on a page via a script. W3C, however, has not approved the Document Object Model as of this writing. A preliminary version of the model is currently up on the W3 site; it reads:

> The Document Object Model is a platform- and language-neutral interface that will enable programs and scripts to dynamically access and update the content, structure, and style of documents. The document can be further processed and the results of that processing can be incorporated back into the presented page.

Now what about dynamic HTML, the lowercase approach? It's slightly simpler: dynamic HTML is the means to manipulate the look, feel, and content of a page by using HTML-based elements like style sheets and layers (another new HTML concept you'll learn about in a few paragraphs) and basic scripts. This differs from using a CGI script to generate content. CGI scripts can build a page based on a set of proscribed data, or in response to user input. Dynamic HTML pages can build a page based on style sheets or layers, then alter the look of the page or the content based on HTML or scripting embedded within the HTML.

Style Sheets

One of the first tools you'll need to master if you want to try your hand at dynamic HTML (or Dynamic HTML) is the style sheet. Style sheets work like this: a group of characteristics are put together and defined as a class. When you find a part of the page where you want to display these characteristics, you enclose it in HTML tags that call the class.

You've decided, for example, that all graphic captions will be small, sans serif type, font weight bold, and bright blue. You've also decided that you want the text to be aligned to the right. You would then draw up a style that defined the class "caption" and specify all items in class caption to have the following attributes.

Table 8.2   Assigning Style Sheet Attributes

Common Description	Style Sheet Tag	Value
small text	font-size	8 point
sans serif type	font-family	arial, helvetica
bold text	font-weight	bold
bright blue color	color	#0000FF
right-aligned text	text-align	right

The beauty of style sheets is that you can control the appearance of a web in much more precise terms: you've got an 8-point font, but what's to say the letters don't look a little squished? You can set the line-height attribute and give your lines 12-point leading if you want.

> **NOTE**
>
> **For you non-fontophiles, leading is the height between the baseline, or bottom line of a line of text, and the baseline of the line of text above or below it. Baselines are the typographic equivalent of the blue lines on a sheet of notebook paper: everything lines up on them and some items, like the tails of the lowercase "g," hang below. The short typography lesson is over.**

You can set margins, you can specify background colors—style sheets enable you to set up a distinctive look and feel for an entire site. All you have to do is define classes for the different elements on the page and remember to insert calls to the classes where they are needed.

A Brief Style Sheet Primer

Style sheets are still a little buggy, but will hopefully even out by the time Netscape and Microsoft release the final 4.0 versions of their browsers. Let's start with how documents can call style sheets, move on to how styles can be called within a document, and then focus on two different types of style sheets. Don't be fazed by the semicolons or syntax within style sheets—it will all make sense soon.

Style sheets can exist independently of or embedded in the middle of an HTML document. The three main ways HTML documents can reference style sheets are:

- ❖ Inline style sheets
- ❖ Embedded style sheets
- ❖ Linked style sheets

Inline Style Sheets

Inline style sheets are employed when the web author takes a set of specific style attributes and attaches them to individual HTML tags within the document. If you wanted to make your bold blue caption an inline style sheet, you might have something like this:

```
<P font-face: arial, helvetica; color:#0000FF; font-weight:bold;>Photocaption
➥goes here</P>
```

You should keep a couple things in mind when using inline style sheets. One important thing to remember is that every time you include style sheet attributes in a document, you must close the tag that calls the attributes, or else the entire document will inherit the attributes. Another thing to keep in mind is that the style only applies to the text within the <P></P> tags. If you have six captions on a page, this might not be the most efficient way to set a document. Inline style sheets are best used for tweaking individual elements or if you're using few styles.

Embedded Style Sheets

With embedded style sheets, the different style classes are all defined in the head of an HTML document, and called within the document. Returning to the blue caption example from the previous section, assume you have five picture captions on a page. You'd write your embedded style sheet like this:

```
<HTML>
<HEAD><TITLE>blue captions</TITLE>
<STYLE TYPE="text/css">
<!--
.caption {        font-size:                8 pt;
            font-family:            arial, helvetica;
            font-weight:            bold;
            color:                  #0000FF;
            text-align:             right;
}
-->
</STYLE>
</HEAD>
<BODY>
<P CLASS="caption">photo caption goes here</P>
```

```
<P CLASS="caption">photo caption goes here</P>
<P CLASS="caption">photo caption goes here</P>
</BODY>
</HTML>
```

Don't let the unfamiliar syntax throw you; the important things to notice here are the following:

❖ The style sheet is defined and enclosed within the head of the tag. The comment lines are there so that older browsers will ignore the style sheet instead of displaying it as gory ASCII text.

❖ The class is the only indication within the HTML document that there's a style attached to the elements. It's a lot more efficient than cutting and pasting the same string of specs into <P> tags. It's also a lot easier to modify. If your boss should nix the blue captions in favor of lime green, all you have to do is rewrite the color #0000FF to read color #00FF00.

Linked Style Sheets

Linked style sheets are the most elegant solution for a large site. In this case, the style sheet is an entirely separate document, and the HTML document that uses the styles refers to the document in two different ways—once in the header, and then every time the author wants to apply a class to the element. Returning to the blue caption example one more time, the style sheet document would look like this:

```
.caption {      font-size:          8 pt;
          font-family:        arial, helvetica;
          font-weight:        bold;
          color:              #0000FF;
          text-align:         right;
          }
```

For example purposes, this code will be saved as caption.css. The HTML that calls the style sheet would look like this:

```
<HTML>
<HEAD><TITLE>linked blue caption</TITLE>
<LINK REL=style sheet type="text/css" HREF="caption.css" title="caption">
</HEAD>
<BODY>
<P CLASS="caption">photo caption goes here</P>
<P CLASS="caption">photo caption goes here</P>
<P CLASS="caption">photo caption goes here</P>
</BODY>
</HTML>
```

This code tells the browser that the page references a style sheet link, what the link is, and what style sheet class to apply to the stuff on the page.

This type of style sheet is most powerful on large sites where you can change an element on hundreds of pages just by modifying the class that the element is calling on that one style sheet. This type of style sheet also lends itself to the most obvious interpretation of the phrase Cascading Style Sheets.

You can link to many different style sheets within the same document, thus cascading style sheets one on top of the other. The other way to interpret the phrase Cascading Style Sheets is to remember that styles can be imported (linked), and the most recently imported style can cascade on top of another, adding to—or overwriting—the previous style. Keep in mind that imported style sheets do not override any styles that you've set up in the document.

Incorporating Style Sheets into Web Pages

Three different ways exist to incorporate style sheets into your document as a whole, and three different ways exist to call a style sheet tag. They are as follows:

❖ **<DIV></DIV>:** The syntax for this tag is `<DIV CLASS="foo">text or object</DIV>`. The <DIV> tags are containers for block-level elements. Block-level elements are those that specify and contain a large amount of text, and are containing it for a reason. A <BLOCKQUOTE></BLOCKQUOTE> is a block-level element. <DIV> tags are great for setting up a document-wide style, and they include a line break after the closing tag.

❖ **<SPAN></SPAN>:** This is the text-level way of calling a style. There is no line break after a </SPAN> tag. This paired tag is best used to apply a new style within a <DIV> container.

❖ **Any HTML attribute:** It is true, you can call a class from a style sheet or define one via inlining by using any HTML element such as <H1>, <P>, or <blockquote>. This enables you to easily see how different styles will carry out across text and block-level elements, but doesn't enable you to easily determine the stretch of your style sheets the way a <DIV> or <SPAN> tag does.

Something that you might want to keep in mind is that although the difference between block-level elements and text-level elements might seem nitpicky, it's a good distinction to draw. Block-level elements define large chunks of content, and they are structurally determined. Text-level elements do not affect the structure of the document; they affect the appearance of one of the items within a block. The following code illustrates this distinction:

```
<BODY>
<B>Headline</B><P>
text text text text
text text text text
text text text text text text text
text text text text
text text text text
text text text text text text text
text text text text
text text text text
text text text text text text text
</BODY>
```

Everything within the <BODY> tags belongs to one block, but the bold tags are text-level elements within the block.

Okay…you know there are three different ways to reference a style sheet on the document level and there are three different ways to call a style on the HTML level. Now let's move on to the syntax of the style sheet itself.

Style Sheet Syntax

Two different types of style sheets are Cascading Style Sheets and JavaScript style sheets. JavaScript style sheets will not be discussed here because at the time of this writing they were not supported by the W3C specs.

Cascading Style Sheets have a specific syntax, and they're rather fussy if you don't follow it. Fortunately, the syntax is easy to learn. Every part of the following code is explained here.

```
.classname        {       attribute : attribute value;
                        attribute : attribute value;
                        attribute : attribute value;

                  }
```

The following bulleted list dissects each part of the Cascading Style Sheet syntax:

❖ **.classname:** Always preface classname with a period. Some exceptions exist, but we're not going to get into them. The classname gives the groups of attributes a name with which they can be referenced later.

❖ **{}:** All the attributes in a style are enclosed within curly brackets.

❖ **attribute:** This is the name of a specific appearance modification to be defined. For a list of the most common attributes, see the handy chart later in this section. Note that all attributes cue the browser for their attribute values by ending with a colon.

❖ **attribute value;:** This is the set value for an attribute within a style. Note that it always ends with a semicolon.

Resurrecting the blue caption example one last time (if *Jaws* can come back four times, why can't one harmless caption?), let's look at the .caption style:

```
.caption { font-size:        8 pt;
          font-family:      arial, helvetica;
          font-weight:      bold;
          color:            #0000FF;
          text-align:       right;
          }
```

The classname here is caption, and five style elements are defined. The values for each style element are listed to the right, and all the statements end in semicolons. Remember that syntax must be exact or the style sheets will not work. (I have spent a lot of time staring at a screen and muttering dark threats to my HTML only to realize I hit the wrong key by mistake and typed l instead of a semicolon in the middle of a style sheet.)

Style sheets are a great way to fine-tune a page's appearance, and best of all, they force you to mentally separate structural HTML from formatting. Even if you're inlining styles left, right, and center, you'll remember that those styles are modifying the appearance of a structural part.

Guide to Style Sheet Properties

A lot of different style sheet properties exist. Table 8.3 is a handy guide to the more common style sheet properties and how they function within HTML code.

Table 8.3   Style Sheet Properties

Style Sheet Property	Functionality
'background'	The most basic of background tags, 'background' is rarely used alone and is used as a cue that a value is attached to the background appearance.
'background-attachment'	Determines if your background image scrolls with the rest of your page, or stays fixed as the rest of your content scrolls over it.
'background-color'	Sets the background color.
'background-image'	Specifies a background image.
'background-position'	Sets exactly where to apply the background image relative to the rest of the page. With a few carefully written and tested pages, you could position four different backgrounds in four different parts of the page.
'background-repeat'	Determines whether or not the background image will repeat and how many times.
'clear'	Determines whether or not a particular element will allow other elements to float to either side of it.
'color'	Sets the color value for the style. It's used most commonly with text styles.
'float'	Sets whether or not you can wrap text around an element. It could be a good way to rid your site of those <IMG ALIGN> kludges.
'font'	The übertag for all font-related tags (like the background tag in that respect) in that it warns the browser that some more specific styles are on their way.
'font-family'	Specifies a particular font or font group.
'font-size'	Sets the size of the font in points, pixels, or percentage.
'font-style'	Specifies that your font is displayed in normal, oblique (slanted), or italic.

Style Sheet Property	Functionality
'font-variant'	Specifies whether you want to display the text in small caps, or normally (lowercase and uppercase).
'font-weight'	Sets the font weight—light and bold are the relative values, but you can also insert numbers for an absolute weight.
'height'	Sets the height of the area within the style tags. You could, for example, decide that the caption has a height of 10 percent (relative) or 120 px (absolute).
'letter-spacing'	Controls how far apart the letters within a chunk of text are.
'line-height'	Controls leading—you can set the line height and prevent squished text.
'margin'	Warns the browser that more specific margin values are on their way.
'margin-bottom'	Sets the bottom margin.
'margin-left'	Sets the left margin.
'margin-right'	Sets the right margin.
'margin-top'	Sets the top margin.
'text-align'	Aligns the text along a horizontal axis.
'text-decoration'	Sets whether you want text underlined; at last, the "turn off the linking option" on web page notices can go.
'text-indent'	Specifies a first-line indent.
'text-transform'	Enables you to exercise three different style options: capitalize the first character of each word, capitalize all characters of each word, or use small letters for all characters of each word.
'vertical-align'	Aligns text along a vertical axis. This is the equivalent of a tables valign= tag.
'width'	Specifies the width of the area covered by the style.
'word-spacing'	Specifies the space between words in a selected area.

Layers

Layers are a second approach to dynamic HTML. They act as containers within a web page, subsequently enabling you to group elements together and assign formatting properties to those elements. Layers differ from Cascading Style Sheets in that they act as containers *on* a page rather than modifying elements *to* a page.

267

In figure 8.1, the large, outer rectangle is the entire HTML document and the embedded, overlapping rectangles are layers that are contained within the document. Note that each layer is a self-contained entity, but you can have layers overlapping.

Figure 8.1

A visual representation of layers.

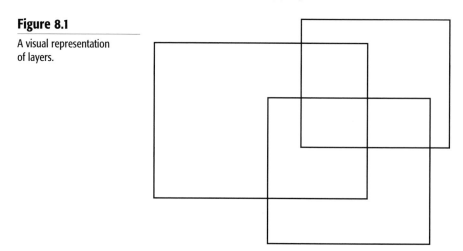

Just as the Document Object Model is Microsoft's baby, layers are Netscape's baby. Layers are not supported by the W3C as of this writing, but Netscape 4.0 promises to support them. It might be a good idea to learn layers for the following reasons:

❖ Layers enable you to set up the precise physical coordinates of an element on your web page.

❖ Layers enable you to precisely control the length and width of an element on your web page.

❖ Layers enable you to change the background color of an element on a web page—no more relying on tables to add blocks of color to your page.

❖ Layers enable you to import another file within a layer. If you were to set up a page so that the navigation bar fits within one layer and the contents of a lengthy article were positioned within another layer, you could call that lengthy article via <A HREF> within the layer, and cut all that HTML out of your formatting page.

❖ Layers provide another approach to dynamic HTML.

❖ The W3C has been known to support browser-driven innovations.

The layer syntax is fairly straightforward: <LAYER></LAYER>, with any content in between. The <LAYER> tag has a number of attributes, all that can help you refine the appearance of the element contained within the layer, without affecting the functionality. The attributes for the <LAYER> paired tag are listed and described in table 8.4.

Table 8.4   Understanding <LAYER> Attributes

Attribute Tag	What Does It Do?
<LAYER></LAYER>	These are the container tags for the elements to be contained within the layer. The idea is to stick the structural stuff inside a layer and set up the formatting via the attribute tags.

Attribute Tag	What Does It Do?
ABOVE	ABOVE="layername"
	The order that layers appear on a web page can be determined by telling the browser that a layer is above or below another layer. You can use only one of these order tags—ABOVE, BELOW, or Z-LAYER in the attributes for a given layer.
	In the case of the ABOVE tag, this tells the browser which layer should appear on top of the layer in whose tag this ABOVE appears. If you have two layers named abbott and costello and you decided that abbott was to lay on top of costello, you'd write costello's tag like this:
	<LAYER ABOVE="abbott">
	Or use my forehead-slapping mnemonic device:
	<the **LAYER ABOVE** me="abbott">
BELOW	This tag tells the browser the name of a layer to place underneath the calling layer. Returning to our abbott and costello example, if you decided you wanted abbott to lay beneath costello, you'd write:
	<LAYER BELOW="abbott"> as costello's layer tag.
Z-INDEX	Remember in trigonometry when graphing shapes moved into that weird Z-INDEX and you wondered if this stuff was ever relevant in the real world? Well now you know.
	The Z-INDEX is the axis that stacks layers on top or beneath each other. A Z-INDEX value is always a positive integer (another trig class flashback!). A z-layer value of 0 places the layer on the "bottom" of the z-axis, a layer with a z-layer value of 1 sits on top of the first layer, a layer with a z-layer value of 2 sits on top of the layer with a value of 1…and so on. If you have three layers—let's call them larry, moe, and curly—and you write:
	<LAYER Z-INDEX=1> for moe
	<LAYER Z-INDEX=2> for curly
	<LAYER Z-INDEX=3> for larry, then larry's on top of the pile, and moe's at the bottom.
NAME	The <NAME> tag is an id label for a particular layer. No two layers within the same document can have the same name. The <NAME> tag comes in handy if you're trying to keep track of all your layers, or if you're planning on using JavaScript to swap layers in and out of a page.
LEFT	<LAYER LEFT="0">LEFT refers to the upper left-hand corner of the layer. This tag enables you to set up the horizontal coordinates of the entire layer by filling in a pixel value or a percentage.

continues

269

Table 8.4 Continued

Attribute Tag	What Does It Do?
	<LAYER LEFT="10%"> tells the browser to place the layer approximately ten percent of the browser window away from the upper left-hand corner of the browser.
	<LAYER LEFT="10"> tells the browser to place the layer approximately ten pixels away from the upper left-hand corner of the browser.
TOP	<LAYER TOP="0"> TOP refers to the top of the browser window; this tag enables you to set up the vertical coordinates of the layer by filling in a pixel value or percentage. Like the LEFT tag, the percentage value places the layer at a value relative to the size of the window, and the pixel value places the layer at an absolute coordinate, window size notwithstanding.
WIDTH	<WIDTH="0"> This sets the width of the layer; like TOP and LEFT it can be a percentage or a pixel value.
	<LAYER WIDTH="80%"> tells the browser to make the layer 80 percent of the browser window size, and <LAYER WIDTH="80"> tells the browser to make the layer 80 pixels, no matter what the browser window size.
CLIP	This tag enables you to set visible parameters on your layer.
	The best way to explain it is to illustrate with an example. Say that you have a picture of your boss and a notorious ex-colleague on a layer. The picture is approximately 200 pixels wide and 100 pixels tall, and the layer has a width of 200 pixels. You notice the boss on the left, and decide that clipping the layer will save you the trouble of altering the picture.
	You notice the boss takes up approximately 125 pixels of the 200 pixel width, and the whole height of the picture. You could write
	<LAYER CLIP="0,0, 125,100">
	That tells the browser to display the layer from the upper-left corner coordinates of 0,0 down to the lower right-hand coordinates 125,100. Your boss shows up, but the ex-colleague does not.
	You could also write <LAYER CLIP="125,100"> and the browser would assume the first set of coordinates is 0,0. The shorthand won't work if you want to show a part of the layer that doesn't begin in the upper left-hand corner—so get in the habit of specifying both sets of coordinates.
visibility	<VISIBILITY=hide>
	<VISIBILITY=show>
	<VISIBILITY=inherit>

Attribute Tag	What Does It Do?
	These are the three choices for this tag. <VISIBILITY> tells the browser whether or not the layer should be shown to the viewer. The inherit tag draws on an interesting phenomenon: layers can nest one inside the other, and the child layer (the nestee) inherits some of its traits from its parent layer. In this case <VISIBILITY=inherit> would tell the browser that the child layer has the same visibility—shown or hidden—as its parent.
BACKGROUND	<LAYER BACKGROUND="image.gif">
	This tag enables you to call in a file to act as the background gif. Imagine the fun you could have with three layers and three different background patterns.
BGCOLOR	<LAYER BGCOLOR="#hexvalue">
	You can set the background color of a layer with this tag. It is this tag that enables you to begin setting apart different HTML elements without having to cram them into a table.

Actually writing layers isn't nearly as difficult as it appears. Let's walk through the code that makes up the page in figure 8.2.

Figure 8.2

This is an example of a document built with several different layers.

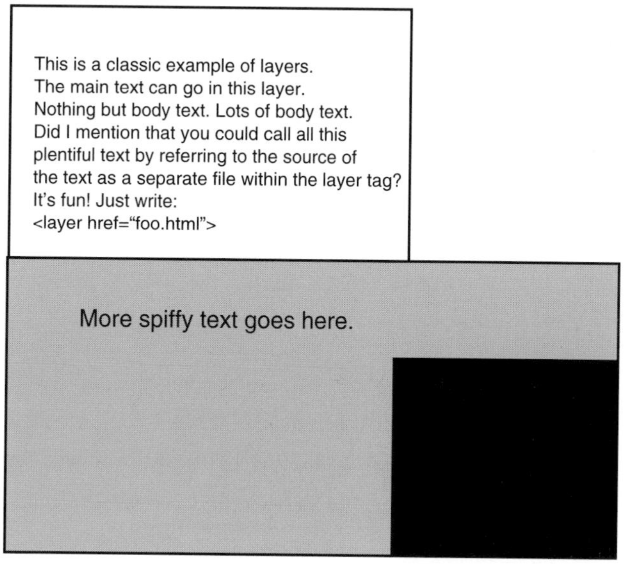

This is a classic example of layers.
The main text can go in this layer.
Nothing but body text. Lots of body text.
Did I mention that you could call all this
plentiful text by referring to the source of
the text as a separate file within the layer tag?
It's fun! Just write:
<layer href="foo.html">

More spiffy text goes here.

```
<HTML>

<HEAD><TITLE>layers sample></TITLE></HEAD>

<BODY>

<!--this sets up the white canvas that the three objects you see sits on-->

<LAYER NAME="canvas" WIDTH=100% LEFT=0 TOP=0 BGCOLOR="#FFFFFF">

<!--this sets up the white text box on the upper left-->
```

271

```
<LAYER NAME="whitebox" WIDTH=200 LEFT=10% TOP=%10 BGCOLOR="#FFFFFF">
<FONT FACE="arial, helvetica" SIZE=1>This is a classic example of layers.
The main text can go in this layer.
Nothing but body text. Lots of body text.
Did I mention that you could call all this
plentiful text by referring to the source of
the text as a separate file within the layer tag?
It's fun! Just write:
<LAYER HREF="foo.html">.</FONT>
</LAYER>
<!--this sets up the gray box-->
<LAYER NAME="graybox" WIDTH=450 LEFT=10% TOP=50% BGCOLOR="#CCCCCC">
<CENTER><FONT FACE="arial, helvetica" SIZE=+3>More spiffy text goes here.</FONT>
➥</CENTER>
<!--this sets up the black box-->
<LAYER NAME="blackbox" WIDTH=100 LEFT=70% TOP=50%>
<!--insert photo or big black gif in here-->
</LAYER>
<!--close graybox-->
</LAYER>
<!--close canvas-->
</LAYER>
</BODY>
</HTML>
```

The following points warrant mentioning:

❖ Layers do not have to contain all the attributes outlined earlier. The ones listed previously only had name, position, width, and background color.

❖ Layers can be nested one within the other. The nested layers are considered children of the layer outside it. Note that these children layers have to live inside the <LAYER> tags, which is why the canvas layer tag is the last thing to close in the previous example.

❖ You can mix percentages and pixel values within layers and within documents.

❖ Notice that positioning is influenced by whether the layer is a child layer. If the layer stands on its own, it's positioned relative to the browser window. If the layer is the child of another layer, it's positioned relative to its parent. This is illustrated in the black box layer. For the black box layer, the top left-hand corner is the top-left corner of the gray layer, so it is placed to the left of that corner, not 70 percent to the left of the browser corner.

Layers can be manipulated and moved via JavaScript. You could, for example, move the black box to the left by dragging-and-dropping, or have something new appear in that box whenever a user mouses over it. JavaScript adds the dynamic portion to dynamic HTML. It adds functionality. Layers are great containers for formatting content without affecting the structural presentation of the information.

Virtual Includes/Server-Side Includes

Server-side includes and virtual includes are the non-style sheet, non-layers alternative to producing and updating a large site. They do this by treating different parts of your web page as separate files, and then call the files in order when the page is loaded.

You have a web site with many pages, for example, all which are composed of the following parts: logo, body copy, navigation bar, and related links. You want to make sure the related links section appears on every page, but the list of links changes every two weeks. Instead of resigning yourself to a lost Friday night once every two weeks, make the links section a separate file, and reference the file in the relevant web pages. When a web page with the file reference (include) is loaded, it will also call the include, and the include's contents will be loaded as well.

Figure 8.3 is meant as a simple symbolic representation of how server-side includes appear on a web page. The HTML file is the black square. When it is called, it calls the SSI files (the remaining shaded squares), and the end result has content from all three files.

Figure 8.3

A graphic representation of how server-side includes appear on a page.

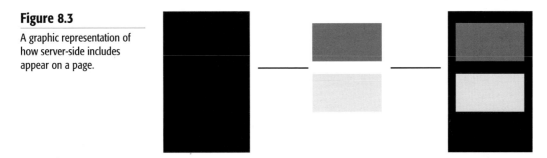

Server-side includes enable you to swap large portions of HTML in and out of your web site, and to modify a web site element that appears on hundreds of pages just by changing HTML in one file.

Server-side includes require some coordination with your Webmaster. You'll need to set up directories that recognize and respond to SSI syntax. You will also need to make sure that the server recognizes the file extension of the files that you want to parse as SSIs. Your includes will have HTML syntax, and will work in an HTML document, but they are not HTML. Therefore, the server handles them differently, converting the files from MIME type to client HTML. Some web servers are set up to parse .html includes, but others prefer to call them .shtml files.

There's also a traffic consideration. The web server parses the documents on-the-fly, and this could have some unsavory results if your server traffic is really heavy.

If you can resolve the technical questions with the Webmaster, you may want to try and incorporate server-side includes into your web site. Virtual includes, which are the most basic type of SSI, can make your job easier for the following reasons:

- ❖ They're more widely supported than style sheets.
- ❖ You can write portions of complex HTML and call them as virtual includes. This makes tweaking your HTML or altering the appearance of elements easier.

❖ You can make your web pages more lightweight. Rather than write hundreds of lines of HTML, just call a few virtual includes within your document.

❖ You don't need to use any kind of scripting to call the virtual includes—it's all HTML and server functionality.

❖ Best of all, the syntax for a virtual include is simple, as shown in the following line of code:

```
<!--#include virtual="filename.shtml"-->
```

All you have to do for virtual includes is write a line, commented out, that contains the `#include virtual`, the name of the file, and the file extension that you and your Webmaster have agreed to for SSIs.

Note that virtual includes appear where they're called, so if you want to call the bottom navigation bar as a virtual include, you'd write HTML that looked like this:

```
<HTML>
<HEAD><TITLE>virtual include example</TITLE></HEAD>
<BODY>
your body copy goes here
<!--#include virtual="bottomnav.shtml">
</BODY>
</HTML>
```

Here's how the web page will appear to the user, after the includes have been called and read.

Figure 8.4

This is a symbolic representation of a page built from server-side includes.

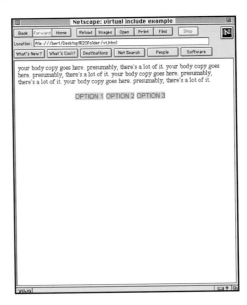

The code for the virtual include bottomnav.shtml is as follows:

```
<CENTER>
<TABLE BORDER=0 CELLSPACING=5 CELLPADDING=0>
<TR>
```

```
<TD BGCOLOR="#CCCCCC"><FONT FACE="arial, helvetica" size=+1><A HREF="#">OPTION
➥1</A></FONT></TD>

<TD BGCOLOR="#CCCCCC"><FONT FACE="arial, helvetica" size=+1><A HREF="#">OPTION
➥2</A></FONT></TD>

<TD BGCOLOR="#CCCCCC"><FONT FACE="arial, helvetica" size=+1><A HREF="#">OPTION
➥3</A></FONT></TD>

</TR>

</TABLE>

</CENTER>
```

Note that the <HTML> or <BODY> tags do not include virtual include tags.

CGI-Bin Scripting

Throughout this book, we've focused on web sites as products comprised of several functional components, and we've worked on writing HTML to make constructing and arranging those components as efficient as possible. CGI scripting takes the web page-as-parts model and pushes it to the next level of efficiency.

How does CGI scripting do this? Start with the basics: CGI stands for Common Gateway Interface. It's the area that mediates between the client (the guy surfing the web) and the server (the machine where the web page being surfed lives). The CGI script passes information back and forth. It's how web pages mysteriously know what domain you're logging in from or what browser you're using. The server takes the information from your query and spits out an answer in response.

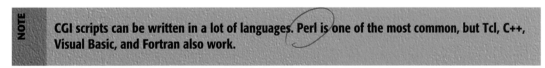

> **NOTE**
>
> **CGI scripts can be written in a lot of languages. Perl is one of the most common, but Tcl, C++, Visual Basic, and Fortran also work.**

The same data-response model works well on web pages too. CGI scripts are executed in real time, so the content can be generated on-the-fly. The following bulleted list illustrates some of the basic advantages that CGI scripts provide you with as a web developer:

❖ You can spit back pages optimized for a client's browser.

❖ You can take virtual includes one step further and write a script that calls several little objects to present a finished page on-the-fly.

❖ You can take client input from a form, pass a few variables, and create a page that is a response to all those variables.

The scripts should live in a designated cgi-bin directory. This serves two purposes. It tells the web browser to execute the CGI script instead of displaying it to the world as a lump of ASCII, and it cuts back on security risks. CGI scripts are risky. They're executable, so it's like letting a random *p. 202* person sit down in front of your computer and run programs. You want to reduce this risk by

275

limiting executable functionality to a strictly defined area, and making sure only the Webmaster can add scripts to that strictly defined directory.

> **TIP**
>
> **If you're using server-side includes like virtual includes, make sure that your /cgi directory has the include option turned off. Otherwise you run the risk of someone hacking your scripts based on information passed via the include. It is a good idea to keep your /cgi directory strictly separate from any content directories.**

CGI scripts emphasize the functionality of the page content—information and active interaction between the information and the user—rather than the presentation of content. They also rely on solid programming skills instead of HTML. CGI scripts are a good way to generate basic pages, or pages where the different layout elements are defined and written as separate objects, or pages that depend on user input. They're efficient if your site depends on queries or client-supplied data. But they're not necessarily the best tool for creating a web site from the ground up. CGI scripts really shine at adding functionality and streaming production on existing content and presentation. For a thorough understanding of CGI scripting, you might want to pick up a copy of New Riders's *The CGI Book* by William E. Weinman.

Summary

This chapter was intended to get you thinking about the next step in web development. By now, you should be reasonably familiar with the following topics:

❖ A working knowledge of usability principles.

❖ An idea of building the back of your site to support the content in front.

❖ A myriad of samples to kick-start your creativity when you're blocked.

The rest of the book should provide you with the tools to get started. So what are you waiting for? Put down this book and begin creating usable, large-scale web sites!

A

B

C

INDEX

O

P

Q-R

U-V

W-X-Y-Z

REGISTRATION CARD

Web Design Templates Sourcebook

Name _____ Title _____

Company _____ Type of business _____

Address _____

City/State/ZIP _____

Have you used these types of books before? ☐ yes   ☐ no

If yes, which ones? _____

_____

How many computer books do you purchase each year? ☐ 1–5   ☐ 6 or more

How did you learn about this book? _____

Where did you purchase this book? _____

Which applications do you currently use? _____

_____

Which computer magazines do you subscribe to? _____

_____

What trade shows do you attend? _____

_____

Comments: _____

_____

_____

Would you like to be placed on our preferred mailing list? ☐ yes   ☐ no

☐ **I would like to see my name in print!** You may use my name and quote me in future New Riders products and promotions. My daytime phone number is: _____

New Riders Publishing   201 West 103rd Street ◆ Indianapolis, Indiana 46290 USA

Fax to 317-817-7448

Fold Here

‖‖‖‖

BUSINESS REPLY MAIL
FIRST-CLASS MAIL PERMIT NO. 9918 INDIANAPOLIS IN

POSTAGE WILL BE PAID BY THE ADDRESSEE

**NEW RIDERS PUBLISHING
201 W 103RD ST
INDIANAPOLIS IN 46290-9058**

CH 1—PLANNING

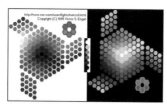

CH 2—PALETTES & WEB

CH 3—TEXTURES

Interface Design
with Photoshop

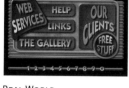

REAL WORLD

CH 13—SLIDERS

CH 12—STOCK IMAGERY

CH 11—3D IMAGERY

CH 10—DISTORTIONS

offers direct step-by-step creation of Web and multimedia interface elements in Photoshop. Each chapter focuses on an important aspect of interface design, including textures, beveling, embossing, and more. With each chapter providing full coverage of one element, you receive all the textual and visual information you need to plan and design interfaces unrivaled by your competition. From the planning stages to creating unique variations, this book will show you how to use Photoshop's power and utilities to your best advantage.

$39.99 USA/$56.95 CAN/
£36.99 Net UK
ISBN: 1-56205-668-9

CH 9—VARIATIONS

CH 4—BEVELING

CH 5—EMBOSSING

CH 6—GLOWS & SHADOWS

CH 7—CHROME, GLASS, PLASTIC

CH 8—BORDERS

Publishing for Professionals

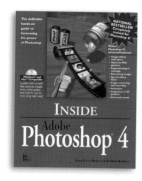

Inside Adobe Photoshop 4

Gary David Bouton

You can master the power of the world's most popular computer graphics program with *Inside Adobe Photoshop!*
Covers Latest Version for Windows and Macintosh
1-56205-681-6 ▲ $44.99 USA/$63.95 CDN ⊙
864 pp., 7 3/8 x 9 1/8, Accomplished - Expert
Available Now

Designing Web Graphics.2

Lynda Weinman

The updated and expanded second edition of this best-selling, full-color, step-by-step guide will teach you the most sucessful methods for designing and preparing graphics for the web.
1-56205-715-4 ▲ $55.00 USA/$77.95 CDN
482 pp., 8 x 10, Full Color, Accomplished - Expert
Available Now

Coloring Web Graphics

Lynda Weinman

This is the essential source that breaks down how to properly use color on the web. The CD-ROM contains over 4,000 ready-to-use electronic browser-safe colors and palettes.
1-56205-669-7 ▲ $50.00 USA/$70.95 CDN ⊙
320 pp., 8 x 10, Full Color, All User Levels
Available Now

Universal Web Design

Crystal Waters

This book is a resource and guide to creating design alternatives on the web. Learn how you can reach more viewers, improve the appearance of your web sites, and enhance your marketability.
1-56205-738-3 ▲ $39.99 USA/$56.95 CDN ⊙
450 pp., 8 x 10, All User Levels
Available April 1997

Chapter 1: The Big Picture: Sending Graphics Over the Web

Chapter 2: The Big Squeeze: Compression

Chapter 3: Bit Depth and Palettes Once and For All

Chapter 4: Molding Images for the Web

Chapter 5: Backgrounds and Texture

About Photoshop
Web Techniques

Chapter 6: Transparency

Photoshop Web Techniques shows you how to harness the power of Photoshop as a web graphics tool. Author Scott Hamlin comprehensively covers several Photoshop techniques through hands-on tutorials and real world examples, as well as provides several "Beyond Photoshop" sections to show you how to incorporate your graphics into such popular web-based technologies as JavaScript and Shockwave. In 11 full-color chapters, you'll learn everything you need to know about creating web graphics with Photoshop and using those graphics to create web pages that will leave your visitors always wanting more.

$50.00 USA/$70.95 CAN/£46.99 Net UK (inc of VAT)
ISBN: 1-56205-733-2

Chapter 7: Working with Text

Chapter 8: Bullets and Buttons

Chapter 9: Imagemaps: The Old and the New

Chapter 10: Creating Images for Shockwave Files

Chapter 11: Web Animations with Photoshop

Paint Shop Pro WEB Techniques

Competition on the web runs high, and in order to compete, you have to know how to create. Web graphics are essential elements of great web pages, and more users are discovering Paint Shop Pro as a powerful tool for creating eye-catching web images. With *Paint Shop Pro Web Techniques*, you'll learn to use Paint Shop Pro to create images and achieve effects you never thought possible. Awarding-winning web designer T. Michael Clark takes you through step-by-step tutorials that show you how to maximize the use of Paint Shop Pro as a truly competitive web graphics creation program. In nine full-color chapters, you learn about color choices and graphics quality, backgrounds and borders, how to create stunning titles, and how to work with third-party filters. You learn to achieve such effects as embossing, drop shadows, chromes, 3D, bevels... and much more.

$39.99 USA/#56.95 CAN/
£36.99 Net UK
ISBN: 1-56205-756-1

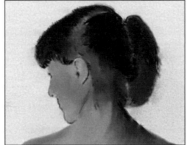

Introduction

Chapter 1 A Brief Overview of Paint Shop Pro

Chapter 2 Color Quality

Chapter 3 Graphics Quality

Chapter 4 Essential Elements of Your Web Page

Chapter 5 Getting Your Message Across

Chapter 6 Backgrounds and Borders

Chapter 7 Filters

Chapter 8 Special Techniques

Chapter 9 Putting It All Together

MACMILLAN COMPUTER PUBLISHING USA

A VIACOM COMPANY

Technical
---- Support:

If you need assistance with the information in this book or with a CD/Disk accompanying the book, please access the Knowledge Base on our Web site at **http://www.superlibrary.com/general/support**. Our most Frequently Asked Questions are answered there. If you do not find the answer to your questions on our Web site, you may contact Macmillan Technical Support **(317) 581-3833** or e-mail us at **support@mcp.com**.